michelle mckinney hammond

Sassy, Single, & Satisfied

DEVOTIONAL

HARVEST HOUSE PUBLISHERS
EUGENE, OREGON

Published in association with the literary agency of Alive Communications, Inc., 7680 Goddard Street, Ste 200, Colorado Springs, CO 80920. www.alivecommunications.com

Cover by Koechel Peterson & Associates, Inc., Minneapolis, Minnesota

Cover illustration © Casey Anderson (caseydraws.com); iStockphoto / donggu

SASSY, SINGLE, AND SATISFIED DEVOTIONAL
Formerly titled *Single-Minded Devotion*
Copyright © 2009 by Michelle McKinney Hammond
Published 2012 by Harvest House Publishers
Eugene, Oregon 97402
www.harvesthousepublishers.com

ISBN: 978-0-7369-4698-8 (pbk.)
ISBN: 978-0-7369-4699-5 (eBook)

Printed in the United States of America

12 13 14 15 16 17 18 19 20 / LB-SK / 10 9 8 7 6 5 4 3 2

*To those who have been waiting on God to
reveal His arms in human form…He is ever near.*

*As we revel in His embrace we find the love
we've been longing for and more.*

*Suddenly we find ourselves giving what we've been
searching for and getting it in return.*

Acknowledgments

Perhaps I struggled with this writing because of what it demands—a willingness to embrace where you are while walking in expectancy of God's best for you. Not an easy thing, but when you do, the reward is so great. This is when God visits, pouring out all that He has. He is ever gracious, giving even when He does not receive and loving when He is not loved. He's ever patient in the face of our lack of trust. Heavenly Father, Jesus, and Holy Spirit—how I depend on You. Thank You for ignoring me when I fight You and for loving me in spite of myself. You are my everything.

To my wonderful Harvest House family. We continue the journey together, and it's all good. I love and appreciate you soooo much.

All my family and friends (you know who you are), thank you for putting up with me when I disappear into the black hole of writing. You're always here when I come out, and I am truly grateful!

Contents

From My Heart to Yours

My dear sister,

God has given you all the ingredients for the best love story ever written. So don't wait for someone else to write it! In your personal love story, a ransom is paid for the life of the princess. The dragon is defeated, and the prince rises to glorious and loving power. There is great celebration and rejoicing! And that's just the beginning.

Your story will be filled with joy as your prince sings "My banner over you is love" and takes you to His Father's house for your wedding and the great wedding feast. You are not single after all! You are engaged and waiting for your divine Fiancé to finish the preparations that are even now being carried out. He wants everything to be perfect for your arrival.

Until then, please allow God to perfect you into a delightful bride. And when you get weary of waiting for the marriage celebration, remember He is waiting too!

With love in Christ Jesus,

Michelle

From the very start
there was only you
you alone before the distractions
the distractions of the lust of the eyes
the lust of the flesh
and the pride of life
before me
before it all
there was you
before serpents
and temptation
and beautiful gardens
before there was light
and sky
before the earth was released
from its watery grave
before there was man
before there was me
there was you
you longing for me
to love you
to worship you
to place nothing
before you...

From the beginning God had plans for our lives. Beyond our dreams of success, beyond the things we want to acquire, and beyond marriage. God created us on purpose with specific purposes in mind. As we dedicate our lives to Him and become who He created us to be and do what He created us to do, fulfillment comes. From the beginning, life was designed to be filled with pleasure and all the perks that come with kingdom living—right standing with God; peace and joy in the Holy Ghost; intimacy with Jesus. That is truly living la vida loca!

A life filled with the purpose of God blesses us. Our lives will overflow with abundant love, exceeding all we can ask, or even think of asking, for. And this flows into the people around us too. God loves seeing all He created thriving. This is what glorifies Him best. We are the evidence of His power and glory. I pray that we will walk in that knowledge and reflect His goodness.

The Sureness of the Word

In the beginning was the Word, and the Word was with God,
and the Word was God. He was in the beginning with God.

JOHN 1:1-2 NASB

*Y*ou have my word," he said.

Promises, promises, I thought.

Sure enough he didn't do as he'd promised. I purposed never to trust him again. To do so would only set me up for disappointment. Better not to take the risk. And thus began the dismantling of my faith in people.

People are one thing; God is another. When God says, "You have My word," He is saying, "You have Me, and in Me you will find all you ever want or need." He *is* His word. He can't be separated from it. What He says He must do. He promises to supply all we need as we live for Him. Only in knowing His words and promises can we be sure of who He is and what He will provide.

To know God's Word, the Bible, is to know Him...and to discover more about His amazing love and faithfulness. God never lies. He can't go against the grain of who He is because He is truth. And His truth sets us free to trust and to hope. We can expect that He will do what He said because He always tells the truth. There is no greater or more faithful love than this. We have His Word.

What are your expectations of God? Do you trust Him to deliver what He promises?

———————————— ✠ ————————————

Precious Lord, teach me to rest in Your Word as I wait on You.
Help me to know and trust Your promises. In Jesus' name.
Amen.

Meditations of the Heart

And the Spirit of God was hovering over the waters.
GENESIS 1:2

The image of the statue "The Thinker" has always left me wondering, *What could he possibly be thinking about so intensely?* We'll never know. The answer is locked away in the mind of the artist. However, when I consider what another artist—God—was thinking about as He hovered over the waters that lay beneath the heavens, I dare to offer the thought that He was thinking of us. Even then, with no one or anything else in sight except a globe covered with water, He was looking forward to meeting and fellowshipping with us.

In His foresight, He saw the earth longing to be filled with life...and He saw us longing to be filled with Him. So He prepared a place for us to dwell. A place He could visit and take up residence when we invite Him into our hearts. He who is greatest of all chooses to abide inside us, giving us a life in Him we only dream of before we know Him. This thought takes my breath away...and makes me contemplate God's majesty and omniscience.

Is there a void inside you? What are you attempting to use to fill that space?

———————————— ✠ ————————————

Heavenly Father, in the moments when I grow aware of a void in my heart, help me once again to contemplate Your goodness. Fill my emptiness. Still the chaos and let me rest in You. In Jesus' name. Amen.

A Sure Foundation

In the beginning you laid the foundations of the earth,
and the heavens are the work of your hands.
PSALM 102:25

*M*ake no mistake about who is responsible for who we are. Though we are to use the tools we've been given, the foundation of who we are was set in place by God. We are the work of *His* hands. Getting back to the core of who we are is essential to moving forward with life. To setting the right boundaries. To knowing our purposes and embracing them.

A tree never tries to be anything but a tree. It grows and flourishes where it's planted. It consistently grows the fruit it was created to produce. It doesn't strive to be a flower. It's not trying to be a bird. It is solidly and unapologetically a tree. The same holds true for us. We are God's creation. We grow and flourish where we're planted. We produce fruit in Christ. We are His.

Perhaps the disconnect for some of us is we're not aware of who we are and why we were created...from God's perspective. We struggle with being, with knowing we're significant in the scheme of life. Are we asking, "Who am I foundationally? Who am I as a woman? As a believer? How does my struggle affect my interactions with people? With my decisions? With the places I choose to go?"

We ask, "Who am I at the core of my being?" God knows the answer! All we have to do is ask Him!

Have you explored who you are in Christ? If yes, what did you discover? If not, why not start today?

---- ✳ ----

Dear heavenly Father, reveal Your will for my life. As I seek You, let me find You—and the me I'm supposed to be according to Your design. In Jesus' name. Amen.

The Value of Wisdom

I [wisdom] was appointed from eternity,
from the beginning, before the world began.
PROVERBS 8:23

Sometimes it seems as if God is taking forever to fulfill His promises for my life. And then I'm reminded that before me there was eternity. My lifespan is a small segment in time for an infinite God. God has all the time in the world to bring His purposes to pass.

You and I are bound by time and humanity. Our flesh cries out for what it wants now. But before you and me, there was Wisdom. She was appointed from the beginning and knows that perfection takes time. God's plans for our lives were birthed out of His omniscience, and Wisdom was part of God's big picture plan for us. Before the world began He knew what we would do, so Wisdom was sent to chart our way, to anticipate our mistakes, and to make ways out of what we think are dead ends.

From the beginning God had us in mind. Before we had questions, He answered them. He reaches down and gives us His knowledge to help us navigate through life and reach our destiny—our divine destiny.

What do you wish you'd known from the beginning?

Dear heavenly Father, thank You for Your wisdom that looks ahead and around the corners. Thank You for Your guidance that leads me toward the plans You've had for me from the beginning. In Jesus' name. Amen.

The Life of the Word

The Word became flesh and made his dwelling among us.
JOHN 1:14

The thought of God speaking everything into existence is so monumental! God's Word always existed. As long as there was God, there was His Word agreeing with the intentions of His mind and heart. God's Word came to life and manifested what He harbored within. His Word was the light first illuminating the darkness. His Word was the expression of who He was and what He wanted. His Word was His Son in living flesh. Yes, Jesus was present when God spoke His first "Let there be..." Jesus nodded in agreement and "there was" because God said so.

There is life in God's Word. Every word He speaks is vibrant and alive. Even more powerful is the thought that God speaks over us every day. He is with us from the moment He says, "Let there be life," and we are born. We are made alive. He says, "Let there be healing," and we are made whole. He commands, "Peace be still," and we are comforted by His Word and by the presence of His Word—Jesus Christ.

Jesus came and brought life and healing. In His presence we are complete and ready to go forth as the intentions of God toward us are revealed. "Let there be!"

What do you need God to speak over your life today?

———————————— ❖ ————————————

Dear heavenly Father, thank You for creating me and giving me life. I want to serve and honor You in everything I do. In Jesus' name. Amen.

Standing by Faith

From the beginning God chose you to be saved
through the sanctifying work of the Spirit
and through belief in the truth.

2 THESSALONIANS 2:13

*P*erhaps our ability to stand firm is sometimes destabilized by what we believe the truth to be. If God is good, and every good and perfect gift comes from Him, it stands to reason that our truth is that we have everything that is good and perfect for our lives right here, right now. As we believe this simple truth, God works to refine us, to prepare us for everything He has for us. His plans for our lives may include a special ministry, a mate, an encounter that will save someone's life...the possibilities are endless.

We won't know until we are in the moment...and perhaps even then we won't realize all that is happening. Sometimes only in hindsight can we figure it out. And it really won't matter because we were saved from the fire of hell for God's specific purposes. This is why we must be sanctified (set apart) and made ready.

Are you willing? Because God chose you, you have something to look forward to! So stand firm in your faith and allow God to do the rest.

What do you believe about God? How are you affected by what you believe?

Dear heavenly Father, I stand firm, waiting on You to finish the work You have begun in me. Most of the time I delight in being set apart for Your purposes. When doubts come, help my unbelief. In Jesus' name. Amen.

The Gift of Grace

[God] has saved us and called us to a holy life—
not because of anything we have done but because
of his own purpose and grace. This grace was given us
in Christ Jesus before the beginning of time.

2 Timothy 1:9

God, in anticipation of who we are and who we will become, put grace in place to accommodate our weaknesses. So adamant was He about having a relationship with us that He looked through the telescope of time and prepared a way for Him to receive us. Before we were, He was thinking of us, anticipating saving us from ourselves and drawing us to Him. He delighted in the thought of washing us, sanctifying us, and making us acceptable so we could meet Him. Isn't that amazing?

Oh, to be a fly on the wall! To hear the conversations between God, Jesus, and the Holy Spirit counseling among themselves on how to go about the task of preparing us to enter the hallowed place where They abide.

I've heard many people say they aren't sure what their calling from God is. I believe this is a simple matter. We are all called to live a holy life. That's what directs us to our God-given destiny. It's not in the "doing" that we fulfill His purpose. It's in the "being." In being His and serving Him.

Have you focused on "doing" more than "being"? If yes, how can you change that?

———————————— �֎ ————————————

Dear heavenly Father, help me focus on Your call for my life. I want to be more in You. In Jesus' name. Amen.

The Reward of Understanding

The fear of the LORD is the beginning of wisdom,
and knowledge of the Holy One is understanding.

PROVERBS 9:10

Fear of consequences often guides our actions. We obey out of fear rather than understanding. We worry God will "get us" for doing the wrong thing. Fear is the beginning of wisdom, but wisdom isn't enough. Doing the right thing without understanding leads to resentment as we imagine moments of missed pleasure.

As a child I was afraid to face my mother when I was caught in an act of disobedience. But that fear didn't lessen the pull of the temptation to do what I wanted. It just made me view Mom as a killjoy. As I matured, I understood the rationale behind her instructions and usually obeyed with a more positive attitude. Her commands were for my good.

What God says is always perfect and good for us, but until we understand how blessed and happy He wants us to be, we won't willingly bend to His wishes. When we know His commands ensure our righteousness, peace, and joy, we walk in the confidence that obedience is better than sacrifice. We can say, "Yes, Lord," and enjoy the safe boundaries He sets for us. What do you seek?

What pleasure do you feel God is keeping from you? What do you need to understand?

Dear heavenly Father, forgive me for not always believing Your will is best. Help me understand and joyfully embrace Your purposes. In Jesus' name. Amen.

God's Perfect Timing

He has made everything beautiful in its time. He has also
set eternity in the hearts of men; yet they cannot fathom
what God has done from beginning to end.

ECCLESIASTES 3:11

*H*ave you pondered the idea that God seems liberated by time while we are bound by it? We spend most of our lives anticipating when something is going to happen. If too much time passes, we grow weary and disappointed and question God. Anxiety and mistrust toward Him alters our conversations and changes our dispositions.

None of this distracts God or makes Him move any faster to fulfill our requests and desires. He knows the plans He has for us. He already knows His completed work will be worth the wait. Ah, yes indeed, it will be a beautiful thing. A "good and perfect" thing. We will hang our heads when we see what He purposed all along and berate ourselves for not trusting Him.

How conflicted we are. The Holy Spirit within us rests in God's perfect timing and feels no urgency because of His awareness of eternity. But our earthbound hearts fear running out of time. We wonder what God is up to and why He is taking so long. We can't fathom that God, in anticipation of our joy, will not settle for presenting us with less than a perfect gift. Perhaps that is why we need faith.

What desire do you think God has "taken too long" to answer? Are you truly ready to receive what you asked for?

---

*Dear heavenly Father, forgive my impatience. Help me trust
Your perfect timing as well as Your heart toward me. Today I
choose to wait on You. In Jesus' name. Amen.*

The Pleasure of God

I am God...I make known the end from the beginning,
from ancient times, what is still to come. I say:
My purpose will stand, and I will do all that I please.

ISAIAH 46:9-10

Sometimes we fear God's pleasure will not be ours. Then the war begins—the wrestling match that superimposes our will over His direction. We maneuver, we question, we rail. We finally give way in a defeated heap as our agenda escapes our grip. Oh, the disappointment we feel when our plans are thwarted!

Yes, God's purposes will stand in spite of us. Because He loves us so passionately and is more determined to bless us than we are to receive the blessing, He allows us the liberty of exercising our will. He doesn't look at the ruins around us with an "I told you so" attitude. When we ask, He gently picks us up, cleans us off, and sets us back on the path toward His divine purposes. His goals ultimately prove to be much better than ours.

For some it takes a lifetime to get to the place of surrender to God, to delight in singing "Have thine own way, Lord" and mean it. This is a place of great liberation. A place that is fertile for innumerable blessings to spring forth from God's storehouse. When we release our will, we also invite God to do what He does best—create, bless, and overwhelm us with His goodness.

Are you wrestling with God right now? What will it take for you to let go?

Dear heavenly Father, I've been afraid to surrender this area of my life to You. Forgive my lack of trust. I release the longings of my heart to You. In Jesus' name. Amen.

The Motive of Obedience

This is love: that we walk in obedience to his commands.
As you have heard from the beginning, his command is
that you walk in love.

2 JOHN 1:6

"If you love me, you will keep my commandments." The words of Jesus cut through all my backtalk, rationalizing, bargaining...you know, the ways we try to get around what God has told us to do. Our obedience to God's Word is not a tool for bartering. "Oh Lord, I've been such a good Christian. You owe me..." No, this will never be true. God owes us nothing. In fact, He has already given us everything—His nearest and His dearest, His only begotten Son, to redeem us, to cleanse us, to empower us to do what He asks.

Our way of saying thank You is to love and obey Him. Our obedience is what we owe for what He's already done. And yet God never suggests we are in debt to Him! He simply asks us to obey Him. Even this request is unselfish because obedience is good for us. It profits Him nothing really. Whether we obey or not, God is still God.

If we choose not to follow Him, we will be worse off from the wear and tear of sin. God's commands are good for us because He loves us. As we walk with Him in love, obedience is a natural by-product. The lover never dreams of doing something that would offend the beloved. With no thought of what he or she gets in return, the lover chooses to love by seeking the pleasure of the beloved. God seeks our well-being and happiness.

Have you tried to bargain with God? What was the result?

———————————— ✳ ————————————

Dear heavenly Father, forgive me for the times I've looked for rewards for my obedience. Today I choose to joyfully obey out of love for You. In Jesus' name. Amen.

It Is Finished

He said to me: "It is done. I am the Alpha and the Omega,
the Beginning and the End. To him who is thirsty I will give
to drink without cost from the spring of the water of life."

REVELATION 21:6

God has completed everything that needs to be done for us. From beginning to end He left no stone unturned. No sentence hanging. No loose threads. And now He says, "Come, I've done the work to serve you rivers of refreshing. The price has already been paid. It is done." There is a note of finality to this that suggests there is no need to ponder, wonder, strain, worry, or fear. It's a done deal. Already settled. Taken care of. It's time to celebrate our tomorrows and know that when we thirst for more life, love, comfort, and healing all we have to do is drink.

All our tomorrows have been provided for. Every problem solved. Every question answered. Now is the time to bask in that knowledge. And it costs us nothing. Jesus paid the ultimate price to issue that invitation to us. His life for ours. He gives freely of Himself to everyone who is weary and thirsty from their life quests. He is the oasis in the desert of our hearts. He saw us coming from the beginning. He sees the end of the matter...and all the in between...and reassures us, "It is done." Our lives are already a finished work, though for us it's still continuing.

What do you thirst for? What will satisfy your needs?

Dear heavenly Father, I thirst for love, for life, for so many things. Many times I've sought refreshment in the wrong places. Now I turn to You. Come and fill me with You. In Jesus' name. Amen.

The Purposes of God

For those God foreknew he also predestined to
be conformed to the likeness of his Son,
that he might be the firstborn among many brothers.
ROMANS 8:29

*I*n the midst of worrying what will become of your life and what God plans to do with you, remember this: The primary reason you are here is to be conformed to the image of His Son. That's right. You were created to reflect God. To show the world what He looks like, just as Jesus did when He was here. Before you were conceived, God had you in mind for this purpose above all other things.

Perhaps in the midst of trying to figure out what our lives are supposed to look like, we need to revisit what *we* are supposed to look like first. We are the clothing wrapped around the purposes of God. He is not here for our agendas; we are here for His. As we allow ourselves to be transformed into the image of Christ, we attract everything and everyone that is conducive to us fulfilling this great purpose. Our being literally feeds into the destiny God has for us—what we become, if and whom we marry, where we go in life. As we focus on this one thing—to be like Him—everything else will line up accordingly. This God knew from the beginning.

Where is your focus as you ponder your life? Where should your focus be?

———————————— ✠ ————————————

Dear heavenly Father, sometimes my focus is divided as my heart pursues its longings. Help me focus on Your desire, trusting You to fulfill mine as I seek to please You above all else. In Jesus' name. Amen.

The Glory Within Us

"For I know the plans I have for you," declares the LORD,
"plans to prosper you and not to harm you, plans to
give you hope and a future."

JEREMIAH 29:11

God doesn't stop at making plans for us. He calls us to action! He wants us to cooperate with His Spirit to accomplish His will. We are His arms and heart and are called to do a mighty work for Him. No wonder the enemy of our souls vies for our attention! We will do the work of God or the work of Satan, depending on who we yield to.

And when we fall, God is faithful to forgive and reinstate us so we can get on with His work. In those moments we glorify the Father as we seek to do what honors Him most—fulfilling His purposes on earth. God lets us make His love and power manifest among the people. His crowning glory is that we reflect Him and lift Him up so that people will be drawn to Him.

Did you catch that? People will be drawn to *Him*. Not us. *Him*. Could it be that while we're trying to catch the eye of admirers we're attempting to draw more attention to us than to Christ within us? That we become a distraction from what is the most beautiful part of us, which is the glory of God at home within us? When we focus on bringing God glory, He will glorify us. We get to bask in His light and be beautified by it. When we lift Him up, not only do we draw people to Him, we benefit from all they get from Him—love and life.

Who will you reach out to this week? How will you share Jesus' love?

———————————— ✠ ————————————

Dear heavenly Father, today I choose to answer Your call and silence the shouting of my longings. Be glorified in me. In Jesus' name. Amen.

God's Will for Us

He predestined us to be adopted as his sons through
Jesus Christ, in accordance with his pleasure and will.

EPHESIANS 1:5

James 4:15 says, "You ought to say, 'If it is the Lord's will,' " but when many people say, "God willing," they're really speaking of some occurrence they *hope* will happen. They're saying, "I sure hope God wants what I want." There's doubt in their minds. They aren't sure if what they want will give God pleasure, so maybe God won't deliver.

We don't need to take a hesitant stand when it comes to discerning God's will. He is clear. He wants us as His own. We give Him pleasure. This is the part of His will we can be sure of. All other matters can be measured in light of this fact. What would God want for someone precious enough to Him to be called His son or daughter? The best! Everything He plans and decides for us supports His design for us—to make us better.

According to His foreknowledge of us, He knows how we will fit into His plan, which is so much greater than our individual desires. He calls us to Him. I picture Him smiling the moment we say yes to His invitation. His expansive, glorious smile lights the heavens as the angels applaud in agreement. God's will is complete.

In what areas have you questioned God's will for your life? How will what you desire make you a better child of God?

Dear heavenly Father, as I seek to please You, merge our wills so I can become the child You long for me to be. In Jesus' name. Amen.

In Hindsight

In [Jesus] we were also chosen, having been
predestined according to the plan of him who works out
everything in conformity with the purpose of his will.

EPHESIANS 1:11

I planned to be married by the time I was 25, have my first child at 27, the second one at 29, have a cat and dog, a two-car garage...with nice cars in them, of course. But none of this happened. I cried. I railed over why God wouldn't give me a mate. And yet He knew all the time that His plan was ultimately better for me...and for the people He planned to touch through me. He knew His plan would give me greater joy.

Now I find myself crossing the 50-yard line still single and surprisingly happy. I'm in ministry for God, reaching thousands of people for Him. That still takes my breath away! If you'd told me this 25 years ago, I wouldn't have believed or received it. The passing years have been nonstop excitement and amazement over the things God has done for me and through me. *Who'd a thunk it!* That's all I can say when I look back. Even in hindsight I sometimes can't believe it.

Obviously I didn't think highly enough of God. It took years of walking with Him to discover He has great taste. His designs for our lives are beautiful. Sometimes we're under major construction, but if we trust Him, we're going to be glorious.

What plans do you need to surrender to God today?

———————————— ✤ ————————————

Dear heavenly Father, today I choose Your plans over my own. Help my unbelief. I want what You want for me more than what I think I want. In Jesus' name. Amen.

The Light Within

God said, "Let there be light," and there was light.
GENESIS 1:3

I find it interesting that the first thing God spoke into existence was light. Light is essential to our well-being. We can't move or function well without it. The absence of light can negatively affect our state of mind. I had a friend who suffered from depression. When she bought special bulbs that imitated sunlight, her mood changed! I've even heard the suicide rate is higher in places that are foggy and dark for long periods of time.

We need light, and not just physically. We also need light spiritually. God is that light. All it takes is a word from Him to set captives free, to heal sick bodies, to release minds, to comfort tear-stained souls. If we choose, we can let the sunlight reassure us that God is on the scene and has noticed our predicament. He's given us promises we can stand on. If God can say let there be light and the universe obeys His word, He can also say, "Let there be provision for you" and "Let there be an amazing opportunity, an open door for you." "Let there be joy…let there be peace…let there be deliverance…let there be love." And when He speaks, His will is put into motion.

We are God's children. Perhaps we should speak less and allow Him to speak more?

What do you need God to speak over you today? In what ways does your vocabulary need to change?

――――――――――――― ✠ ―――――――――――――

Heavenly Father, forgive me for speaking words of doubt and indecision. Help me be silent before You so I can listen and understand You better. In Jesus' name. Amen.

The Light of Truth

God saw that the light was good,
and he separated the light from the darkness.
GENESIS 1:4

"The truth is the light, baby," she told me. I wasn't happy. What she said smarted. Never mind that it was true. I wanted what I wanted—now. What I desired wasn't good for me, but so what. And here was my dear friend, loving me enough to tell the truth. Ugh! But she was right. The truth is light, and it was illuminating a dark, slippery path that would have brought devastation to my heart. God's light separates the darkness of deception from our lives and magnifies what is true and right—whether we like it or not.

A friend of mine kept her man under wraps until after she married him because she didn't want anyone's input (a strong sign something wasn't right). The marriage was a disaster. Listening to wise counsel may have saved her from much heartache.

God's Word says we prefer darkness over light because our deeds are evil (John 3:19). Sometimes it's not that deep. What we yearn for may just not be good for us. When we've been wanting something for a long time, the first chance we have to get it can look so good. In those moments, we need to depend on God and the people He puts in our lives to help us separate fact from fiction. We may not like it…but it will be good for us.

Have you been harboring something in the dark? What do you fear if you expose it? What will you do about it now?

———————— ✠ ————————

Father, help me walk in transparency and accountability with You and others, knowing that You will lead me on a straight path to life and joy. In Jesus' name. Amen.

One of the choices on a popular matchmaking website for evaluating the state of a present relationship is, "It's complicated." Perhaps we are the ones who complicate the simple-yet-complex design for relationships that God had in mind. Our needs mirror God's desire for fellowship and intimacy. In the beginning, when man and woman were naked and unashamed, the celebration of love was untainted and deliciously pure. But let's ramp up to present day, and not only are we covered with a load of guilt, shame, and pain, we're also dragging heavy baggage from other relationships that color our outlook on love.

Though we desire relationships, so much stands in the way of us being able to embrace what we desire that it can get complicated. Perhaps a visit back to the garden of Eden is needed to realign our hearts and spirits and get back on track about this thing called love.

Pure Reflections

God said, "Let us make man in our image, in our likeness."
GENESIS 1:26

*G*od wants us to look like Christ. This is a huge thought. We are being transformed to reflect more and more of God's character as we mature in Christ. Our characters, our dispositions, our attitudes can glorify God when He is manifested in our lives daily. From the critical to the mundane aspects of our routines, God shows His strength. This is what makes others hunger and thirst after Him.

I so want to resemble Jesus, don't you? Reflecting Him separates the immature from the mature. To rise above our natural inclinations and take on godly attributes is the cleanest line of demarcation we can draw between ourselves as Christians and the people who refuse to follow Christ. There needs to be something different about us so those who don't know Christ will notice and ask us why. Then we can share who Christ is.

How do we get over ourselves so we are saturated with God's Spirit? Through a passionate relationship with Him. Think of a couple in love who have been together for many years. Eventually they even look related and their exchanges reveal their close relationship. Oh, to peel off the many layers of us until we resemble God so much that others are struck by the similarities! What a fantastic attainment that would be.

What stands in the way of your life revealing God to others?

Dear heavenly Father, let there be less of me and more of You in my life each day. I willingly die to me so more of You will be seen by others to Your praise and glory. In Jesus' name. Amen.

The Perfect Soul Mate

The LORD God formed the man from the dust of
the ground and breathed into his nostrils the breath of life,
and the man became a living being.

GENESIS 2:7

This first encounter between God and man may explain so many things. The exchange of breath, in many ways "a kiss," that imparted life is a spiritual exchange. In the movie *Pretty Woman,* the female lead refused to kiss the leading man. Her explanation was simple. If she kissed him, she would become emotionally involved. A kiss is intimate. In fact, one of the words for worship in Hebrew literally means to "kiss forward," to kiss God in a sense. And when we do that, relationship is established.

Since that intimate, life-giving kiss between man and God, people have been searching for similar experiences. Most of the time we're disappointed because we pursue that intimacy in human relationships. As single women, we long for love so we look to men, who can only offer imitation commitments that fall far short of what God delivers. God is our ultimate Soul Mate. His breath gives us life. God is our primary source for love and meaning. Only He fully satisfies.

Who do you turn to for love and fulfillment? Can people truly satisfy you?

———————————— ❖ ————————————

Dear heavenly Father, far too many times I've looked to others to fulfill what only You can. Please fill me with Your love and presence. Grant me occasional foretastes of our oneness in eternity to give me hope. In Jesus' name. Amen.

The Essence of Kingdom Living

Now the LORD God had planted a garden in the east, in Eden;
and there he put the man he had formed.

GENESIS 2:8

God has made preparations for our pleasure. He created a place for us to enter and experience kingdom living in its fullness. Righteousness—right-standing with Him—peace, and joy in the Holy Ghost await. There is joy that comes from knowing and experiencing the peace that all is well with our souls and that we'll experience God's love for eternity.

The word "Eden" comes from the Hebrew for "delight." It was always God's intention for us to experience pleasure in this life and in eternity. God bookends His Word with positives. We begin in Genesis with man in the midst of God's garden and end in Revelation with us entering His loving presence for eternity.

How do we receive the joy and happiness available in God? And why do they elude us so often? Perhaps because we spend so much time pursuing them we fail to grasp the understanding that only by the hand of God can we be transported to a place of peace and love. Entering God's kingdom is a supernatural event completed by His hand alone. *God* placed the man in Eden.

Are you blocking the happiness God desires for you? Are you brushing aside His hand as He offers what you long for? Why not open your heart and let Him be your joy?

Dear heavenly Father, forgive me for the times I push You away while I pursue pleasure on my own. My heart is open to You. In Jesus' name. Amen.

Our Heavenly Assignment

The LORD God took the man and put him in
the Garden of Eden to work it and take care of it.
GENESIS 2:15

God created us for specific tasks He had in mind before we existed. As we yield to His hand, He places us where He wants us to be so we can do His will. We've been wired for our God-designed assignments. His purposes permeate us and drive our decisions. As humans we get some pleasure and find significance in life on earth because God created us that way. But greater still is the joy and meaning we experience when we seek God and do what He created us to do for Him. Even work-related goals give us satisfaction when we're led by God. I often think of the many people who go to a job they hate. How sad. And many times it's because they've chosen practicality, what "makes sense" or what they've happened upon, over pursuing the talents and gifts God has given them.

God told man and woman to care for His creation, including the garden of Eden. Adam experienced pleasure as he went about his work. I imagine creation cooperating—the earth watered itself and gave forth fruit in abundance. Animals were peaceful, and Adam (and Eve) exercised dominion easily and gently. But when we're not following God's plan, work can become labor...and life gets bleak.

Are you where God wants you? Are you experiencing the pleasure that comes from being in the center of His will?

———————— ✠ ————————

Father, thank You for loving me. Reveal what You want me to do and then help me do it. Let all I do be for Your glory. In Jesus' name. Amen.

God's Design

The LORD God said, "It is not good for the man to be alone.
I will make a helper suitable for him."
GENESIS 2:18

*W*as Adam really alone? No. He was enjoying working in the garden of Eden, living in harmony with creation. And God visited Adam every evening! So why did God say Adam was alone? I believe when we get busy about our Father's business, God gets busy about our personal business. God decided to give Adam someone "of his own kind" to love, to cherish, and to help.

Mates weren't created to be our fulfillment, our affirmation, or our validation. These are God's purview. He created a place in our hearts for Him alone. When we get busy doing what we were created to do, we'll feel satisfied and full of purpose. And God's will and assignments for us always include service of some kind.

God's design for divine partnership is two people coming together to become even more effective in carrying out His kingdom agenda, to give each other company, and to be fruitful. As couples accomplish their purposes, they also find pleasure in one another. This is a wonderful benefit God provides. We have something to look forward to as God prepares us for our mates...and our mates for us. And if God's design for some of us is to remain single, He will provide pleasure and fulfillment in different ways.

What is your assignment now?

Dear heavenly Father, I release my wants into Your hands and wait on what You know I need in my life right now. In the meantime, help me find pleasure in serving You. In Jesus' name. Amen.

The Responsibility of Authority

Now the LORD God had formed out of the ground all the beasts
of the field and all the birds of the air. He brought them to the man
to see what he would name them; and whatever the man
called each living creature, that was its name.

GENESIS 2:19

God allowed Adam to name all the animals. Can you imagine how much fun he had coming up with creative new words? And God honored Adam's choices by not changing the names. The animals' identities were established based on Adam's words.

Many times in life we name situations and people something other than what God would. For instance, is your "Mr. Right" really "Mr. Right"? Or are you seeing him only as you'd like to? Is the choice to stretch the truth—a "white" lie—to avoid trouble really the right one and in line with God's principles? What would God call that situation or choice you've selected?

Until we're ready to see things as God sees them, we'll make choices depending on our moods and attitudes and human reasoning, which often sets us up for pain and regret. Your prince might really be a frog. That great opportunity might be a distraction from a true blessing. A little lie might snowball into a disastrous situation. Look closely and pray about what you're seeing and choosing. Ask God to help you see with His eyes and heart.

What are you calling your present circumstances? What would God call them?

———————————————— ✵ ————————————————

Dear heavenly Father, grant me the discernment and wisdom I need to make the right choices. Help me walk in agreement with You, calling things as You see them. In Jesus' name. Amen.

Finding the Right One

But for Adam no suitable helper was found.
GENESIS 2:20

As Adam named the animals passing him, did he compare himself to them? He did notice all the animals had mates. And that their mates were like...yet unlike...them. They walked together as partners. They fit together. They empowered one another. They nurtured one another. They protected each other. Hmm...not unlike what we want and need from the people we choose to walk through life with.

Adam was also smart enough to figure out that none of the animals were a perfect fit for him. No helper was found for him. Do we recognize what does *not* work for us as well as what *does* when we're considering potential mates? As I mature, I've found I have more clarity about what fits or doesn't fit in my world and what works and doesn't work for me in relationships. No longer do I call frogs "princes."

After we marry, we're to love and serve our mates after the model of how the church and Christ interact. So it's important that we look for people we can admire and respect. We want potential mates to support us and be supportable by us. In finding and selecting the right partners, the right professions, the right choices for our lives, we must begin with expanding our knowledge of God and His Word and exploring our preferences and bents so we can recognize what is suitable and perfect for us.

What are you looking for in a mate? What needs to be evident in your options?

———————————— ✢ ————————————

Dear heavenly Father, show me who I really am and reveal Your plans for me. Teach me how to make the right choices— Your choices. In Jesus' name. Amen.

A Place of Rest

So the LORD God caused the man to fall into a deep sleep;
and while he was sleeping, he took one of the man's ribs
and closed up the place with flesh.

GENESIS 2:21

For so many years I struggled to find a place of rest in my spirit when it came to marriage. Like sleeping on a lumpy mattress, I could never find the right spot or position to get comfortable. There were respites when I was fine with being single, but I always got restless again. I was irritated that this issue wasn't settled…and was so unsettling. And then it happened. I can't tell you how or when…I just finally noticed I was at peace. I no longer wrestled with the big "when will I find a mate and get married" question.

The Bible doesn't say whether Adam ever asked God when he would have someone like the animals seemed to have. What it does say is that the Lord put Adam to sleep. Although this refers to physical rest, it works spiritually too. Resting in God by trusting Him is ultimate surrender. This is when He does the most work to prepare us for the fruitful lives He's planned for us. We can stop trying to make things work. God will bring about what He desires.

In what ways do you need to rest more in God, allowing Him to prepare you for what is to come? What stands in the way of resting in Him?

Heavenly Father, help me find peace in You. I choose to stop striving to make things happen and surrender to Your will and timing. In Jesus' name. Amen.

The Man/Woman Thing

Then the LORD God made a woman from the rib he had
taken out of the man, and he brought her to the man.

GENESIS 2:22

*H*ave you heard this saying? "God made the woman from the rib of man so she would walk beside him and cover his heart." Yes, He carefully formed this amazing creature called Eve. Artfully He integrated Adam into her design and vice versa. She was part of him. Her absence would leave him feeling a great divide. Her presence would make him feel complete.

Perhaps this is where the idea of a soul mate comes from. The feeling of familiarity two people who are meant to be together often feel upon first meeting. The pull can be so strong it's difficult to ignore. A divine connection is made because God is the only one who can design a perfect match.

Adam was placed at rest while God did the work of fashioning the one who would be a "help meet" for him. A woman who would complement Adam, and who Adam would complement, so they could fulfill God's purposes and each other. Eve would be the perfect team player to help Adam complete his God-ordained assignment. Eve wasn't presented to Adam until God was satisfied with her...until she was finished and perfected into a good and perfect gift.

I can think back on the many times I thought I was ready for a mate and now realize I wasn't. God knew it, and now I know it. God, in His wisdom, often constrains us from achieving our dreams until we're ready to be completely blessed and be a complete blessing. And so today I wait and rest, allowing Him to finish what He's begun in me. I'm trusting that at the end of His work He will produce a "good thing"—a beautiful work of art. Can you relate?

---

*Dear heavenly Father, please finish what You've begun in me.
I yield all that I am to You so I can become the blessing You
designed me to be. In Jesus' name. Amen.*

How to Be Chosen

The man said, "This is now bone of my bones and flesh of my flesh; she shall be called 'woman' for she was taken out of man."

GENESIS 2:23

*B*efore God fashioned the woman, He fashioned the man. As Adam named the animals, he was walking within the authority God gave him. He was a man practicing dominion and helping create order in the world around him. By the time Eve was presented to him, he was comfortable naming things. His ability to discern that Eve was bone of his bone and flesh of his flesh came from experience.

Notice Eve didn't wake up Adam. Didn't dash over and say, "Wake up, Adam! God said you are my husband." No, she was recognized, chosen, and named by her man. Everything about Adam and Eve coming together was done in specific order.

The Bible tells us that "he who finds a wife finds what is good and receives favor from the LORD" (Proverbs 18:22). Jesus—the perfect model of a bridegroom who chose His bride (us!), pursued, wooed, and fought to claim her—set the standard for what men are supposed to do. When women reverse the order by pursuing men, they destroy the order God created that lays a firm foundation for fruitful relations between men and women. Men are wired to be hunters. When a hunter gets captured by the game, he will always stand ready to reclaim his position as hunter, usually by setting his eye on other game. This sets a woman up for painful rejection. When a woman is chosen and named by a man, she gets security and a sense of great value.

In what ways can you show you trust God to be Matchmaker in your life?

Dear heavenly Father, I know You are the master Matchmaker. I submit my heart and will to You. I choose to wait for You to present me to the one You have chosen for me. In Jesus' name. Amen.

The Weight of Commitment

*For this reason a man will leave his father and mother
and be united to his wife, and they will become one flesh.*

GENESIS 2:24

Many fail to see the gravity of this thing called "commitment." I've been known to accidentally call weddings "funerals," fully realizing that life as we know it will be irrevocably changed. The refusal to die to the old life and accept the new one is death to a marriage. For those who have committed themselves totally to their mates, the concepts of sacrifice and change are very real.

The apostle Paul said of his Christian journey that at one time he was a child, but as he grew in Christ he put away childish things. This same view needs to be embraced in marriage. Perhaps the romantic vision of marriage that many singles hold keeps them from dealing with the reality of what happens after they utter "I do." As the proof of how different life will be sets in, many couples fail to make it past the period of adjustment.

Marriage is not for the faint of heart. It's a call to sacrifice and change. It's a place where the oneness of the godhead is reflected (through the picture of God, man, and woman) so people will give glory to God for what He is doing in the couple's life together.

The training for selfless living begins with walking with God in our singleness. How we deal with authority in our families, on our jobs, in our activities, and at church reveal where we're at in submitting to God. Our ability to be great mates is only as great as our ability to be surrendered to God. And we leave all we hold dear to be joined to Him.

What areas do you need to surrender to God? What do you still cling to that may hinder your relationship with Him?

Heavenly Father, today I give myself to You completely. Teach me what it means to truly surrender and become one with You. In Jesus' name. Amen.

The Beauty of Transparency

The man and his wife were both naked, and they felt no shame.
GENESIS 2:25

ransparency is a beautiful thing when we have nothing to hide. Ah, but when we do, the thought of having everything visible is frightening. To expose parts of ourselves to people who may not offer or possess the grace to accept us as we are challenges our ability to share who we really are. And yet in all of our relationships, heavenly and earthly, transparency is crucial. We will experience intimacy in proportion to what we're willing to expose.

God encourages us to come to Him, bringing and exposing our sin and shame. "Though your sins are like scarlet, they shall be as white as snow" (Isaiah 1:18). True love covers the weaknesses of the beloved.

This is the beauty of God's grace. In spite of what He sees, He loves us. In His eyes the admission of our failures opens the door to a deeper relationship with Him. Our willingness to press past our shame and come clean with Him lets Him empower us to become greater in every aspect of love and life.

As Adam and Eve encountered one another for the first time, they brought nothing but themselves. No past dramas or negativities that would color their relationship. Allowing God to wipe the slate of our past relationships and interactions clean so we come bearing nothing that hinders the flow of love (whether it's with a mate, coworkers, or friends) is the ultimate freedom. God can restore our innocence and take away our past hurts and shame. God can make us free to love according to His divine design. As we allow Him to do so, we find the peace that comes from His acceptance and grace that allows us to accept others as they are.

What areas of your life do you hesitate to share? What makes you hide these things? What would it take for you to be more transparent?

Dear heavenly Father, I bring all my personal struggles to You. Please restore my life and my heart. Wash me and free me from shame. In Jesus' name. Amen.

The Deceit of Temptation

When the woman saw that the fruit of the tree
was good for food and pleasing to the eye, and also
desirable for gaining wisdom, she took some and ate it.

GENESIS 3:6

Everything that looks good is not good for us. This is an old saying, but it's nonetheless true. Our hearts can lead us down the wrong track, taking us further away from God's will than ever before. Hearts are deceitful, convincing us of untruths that don't agree with the heart of God. "Yeah, go for it! After all you owe it to yourself," is what we often hear. False entitlement creeps in, convincing us of what we deserve.

This sense of entitlement is often part of the conditional love many have toward God. They say, "I've been good; therefore, I should have..." or "Why haven't You given me this yet?" In these moments, the enemy of our souls is offering tasty treats that seem harmless so we eat. But every "good" opportunity isn't a God-ordained opportunity. Every "good" man isn't God's choice for us. An innocent choice can be a sinful one if the wrong motives are attached to it. When we vie for our independence from God, sin is present. In the garden of Eden, the fruit looked good and beautiful. But would it give Eve the wisdom she sought? The apostle Paul said all things were lawful for him, but not necessarily expedient. We need to guard that our choices in life aren't ruled by our desires. They need to be guided by the will of God. What we embrace and eat will become part of us...and in some cases may consume us! So let's be careful what we ingest.

What do you hunger for? Are your desires God-driven or self-driven?

Dear heavenly Father, help me align my will with Yours and trust that You withhold things for my good. In Jesus' name. Amen.

The Contagious Nature of Sin

She also gave some to her husband,
who was with her, and he ate it.

GENESIS 3:6

Sin is contagious. Our thoughts, attitudes, and actions affect people far beyond our personal lives. Think about how one person's actions can affect the way we travel. One bomb in one shoe means most travelers in the world now must remove their shoes for inspection before boarding commercial planes.

What we consume in thought, word, and deed may eat at us and spread to others. Eve's little snack in the garden didn't just affect her. She gave some of the fruit she tasted to her husband, and the entire world paid the price. From mankind to nature, everything suffered because of one sin. Can anything taste good enough to be worth those ramifications? I think not!

Sin boils down to our choices, which must always be considered in the present light and in light of the future. We need to have "kingdom" vision to make the right choices. So our choices must be examined by whether they get us closer to where God wants us to be. Until we master this, we will forever be taking one step forward and two steps back in life, in our relationships, and in our accomplishments.

If we truly want victory in our lives, we must see our choices for what they are and how they affect us and others. Whether it be family members, friends, community, or beyond, our actions affect a lot of people. We influence more than we know. So what can we do to effect change for good? Be careful with our choices.

What is the best choice you've ever made? The worst? What were the fruits of your choices? What did you learn? What, if anything, would you do differently next time?

Dear heavenly Father, help me make the best choices—the ones that align with Your will. I want to be blessed...but also to be a blessing to others. In Jesus' name. Amen.

46 — *Sassy, Single, and Satisfied* Devotional

Outside God's Grace

Then the eyes of both of them were opened,
and they realized they were naked; so they sewed
fig leaves together and made coverings for themselves.

GENESIS 3:7

*I*sn't it interesting that the same thing that caused no angst between Adam and Eve before became an issue after they disobeyed God? The same nakedness that held no shame took on a different tone after they chose independence from God. The need to cover themselves only set in when they willingly excluded God from their decisions and the way they interacted with one another.

Insecurity was born that afternoon in the garden. Yes, independence from God always affects our identities—the way we see ourselves and the way we look at others. Outside the light of God's grace, our nakedness is shameful. So we hide. From God. From ourselves. From one another. Obviously hiding hinders intimacy. And lack of intimacy destroys relationships. Lack of relationships robs us of the joy we long for.

God never willed for us to run for cover. He wants us to experience the freedom that comes with being authentic, approachable, and touchable—all the things that make us truly lovable. And yet so often the real us remains hidden, deflecting the very thing we want: true relationship...true connection, where nothing stands between us and God. Between those we love and us.

Fortunately, any cover we find or devise is temporary at best. Everything will eventually be exposed. We can choose to expose our sins now and ask God for forgiveness or we can wait...letting the resulting conflicts and problems interrupt our relationship with Him and with others.

What are you struggling to conceal? What do you fear? When will you give this to God and ask for His forgiveness?

Heavenly Father, help me be my authentic self. Let my identity be completely open and free of shame in You. In Jesus' name. Amen.

The Right Kind of Fear

Then the man and his wife heard the sound of the LORD God as
he was walking in the garden in the cool of the day, and they hid
from the LORD God among the trees of the garden.

GENESIS 3:8

The idea that our ways are hidden from God is absurd. Where can we run that we escape His vision? Nowhere. Perhaps if we practiced being aware of His presence constantly, our words and actions would change. Absorbing that God is always present, that His eyes are always upon us can be comforting...if we're open and honest and real with Him.

As a child I thought my mother had spies or an extra set of eyeballs that followed me wherever I went. No matter where I was, she always seemed to know what I'd been doing. She would meet me at the door when I got home with a recap of some things I never intended to tell. After a while I got the picture that she was my protection. As I embraced her "all knowingness," it began to guide my choices. I found myself making fewer decisions I would later regret. My obedience dismissed my fear of facing my mother and made home a place I ran to without trepidation.

Though the fear of the Lord is the beginning of wisdom, this kind of fear isn't the kind that keeps us from His presence. It's reverent wonder, being awestruck by this Being who loves us and sacrificed so much for us. Because of all He's done, we joyfully choose obedience to Him. We bare our nakedness before Him without shame and fear. At the end of the day, God sees and knows everything. There is no cover that His eyes of love can't penetrate. So why run? Why not turn to Him, allowing Him to cover us with His love and grace and mercy?

What are you wearing today...and why? Do you need to change clothes?

Dear heavenly Father, I choose to run toward You instead of hiding behind my shame. As I embrace You, let Your grace cover and restore me. Thank You. In Jesus' name. Amen.

God's Search for Us

The LORD God called to the man, "Where are you?"
GENESIS 3:9

*T*rust me. God knows where you are. God is not naïve concerning the ways that you take. His knowledge of your nature and inclinations led Him to the sacrifice Jesus made on Calvary for you.

Why would a God who is all-powerful, all-knowing, and ever-present ask, "Where are you?" The answer to this was glaringly evident. God knew the answer. He was giving Adam an opportunity to fess up and locate where he was and where he needed to be. Adam should have replied, "Here I am, Lord! I'm standing here in need of You." "Here I am, Lord, wretched and broken." "Here I am, Lord, overwhelmed by my weaknesses and need." "Here I am, Lord, needing You more now than ever." "Here I am…"

Where you are is where God will meet you. When we come to the end of ourselves God's faithfulness becomes more apparent. His glory will shine brighter than before.

What are you in need of? Where are you now? Answer these questions truthfully and discover another facet of the brilliance of God's grace.

Dear heavenly Father, here I am, ready to serve You. I love You. In Jesus' name. Amen.

The Shame of Nakedness

[Adam] answered, "I heard you in the garden, and I
was afraid because I was naked; so I hid."
GENESIS 3:10

One night I had a dream that I was wandering aimlessly through a labyrinth that ended in a cavernous room. The room was actually a shower. The water looked so cool and inviting that I disrobed and allowed the water to cascade over me. As I stood there beneath the water, the most beautiful man I'd ever seen entered. As he walked toward me I was overwhelmed by his perfection and even more aware of my nakedness. I was covered with ugly scars from the top of my head to the bottom of my feet. I dropped my head in shame because there was nowhere to hide. I was embarrassed by my desire for him because, after all, no one as beautiful as he was would go for the likes of me.

But still he came. Silently he stood behind me and began washing me. He touched my scars gently. There was healing in his touch. He never asked any questions. He soundlessly continued washing me as I wept. And then he took a huge, white terry cloth robe and engulfed me in it. My sobs reverberated off the walls of the shower as he held me.

I woke with my face drenched in tears. In the silence of the night the Lord spoke quietly. "Michelle, you never have to hide from Me. I am well able to cover you with My loveliness."

At the end of the day we can never cover our nakedness, heal our wounds, and remedy our sinful natures. That is a job for the very One we're running from. Turn to Jesus and run into His arms. Allow Him to become your refuge and kneel before the cross. Yield to His touch and lose your shame beneath His gaze. Come out, come out, wherever you are!

In what ways have you felt exposed? What is the cause of your nakedness?

--------------------------------- ❖ ---------------------------------

Heavenly Father, take me into Your arms and cover me. In Jesus' name. Amen.

In Search of Enough

And [the Lord God] said, "Who told you that you were naked?
Have you eaten from the tree that I commanded you not to eat from?"
GENESIS 3:11

The most elusive thing in life is "enough." God, speaking through Haggai, the prophet, said to the people,

Give careful thought to your ways. You have planted much, but have harvested little. You eat, but never have enough. You drink, but never have your fill. You put on clothes, but are not warm. You earn wages, only to put them in a purse with holes in it (Haggai 1:6).

Though he was referring to the fact God's people had neglected the house of the Lord to pursue pleasure, the same can be said of us. When we make us the priority instead of obeying God, our lack is magnified.

Adam and Eve had no problem being naked until they chose to pursue pleasure they thought God was robbing them of. This is the sticky wicket. The enemy of our souls tries to convince us we lack something, that God is holding out on us. And if we choose to believe this hateful seed, our nakedness becomes magnified. Suddenly our dreams seem out of reach.

Our natural inclination is to grow suspicious and discontent. "Why is God taking so long to give us this?" we ask. Our misery grows until we're confronted by the Spirit of God, who challenges us to give careful thought to our ways. "What fruit have you eaten to absorb so much discontent? What has buried your faith and made you question My intentions?" Then we examine our demands and realize we've gone astray. Praise the Lord that we can confess our errant ways and the Lord will welcome us back!

Do you have enough? Why or why not?

———————— ✠ ————————

Dear heavenly Father, please silence the voice of discontent within me and replace my fears and doubts with Your truth and faithful promises. In Jesus' name. Amen.

The Liberating Power of the Truth

Then the LORD God said to the woman, "What is this you have done?" The woman said, "The serpent deceived me, and I ate."
GENESIS 3:13

I once worked in the field of advertising, writing commercials for many well-known clients. And yes, I was good at it. I was good at crafting temptation. I could sell ice cubes to an Eskimo sitting in an igloo. However, what I learned about the art of seduction was that I had to locate what the person wanted. People are only tempted when they are drawn by their lusts. Temptation never works for the sake of temptation alone. It only works when leveled at a person's desire. A nonsmoker will seldom be tempted by a cigarette ad because they have no desire for a smoke in the first place.

This is why God can't be tempted. God is complete, whole, and entirely satisfied. Everything He wants is already contained within Him. When we allow Him to take up residence in our hearts, we are filled with Him, and He supplies all our needs…when we choose to embrace that realization.

The Lord held Eve accountable for her sin even though the serpent was the perpetrator. The serpent only tapped into Eve's rebellious nature and her desire to be like God. A famous comedian used to say, "The devil made me do it." The joke was that we all knew he wanted to do it to begin with. At the end of the day, when we stand before God, we can't blame anyone else for our actions. We must own what we've done and be willing to come clean. We must repent, let God restore us, and move on. An "admission of guilt" *is not* the same as confession. Only when we see what we've done through the eyes of God and call it as it truly is will His grace finish its perfect work in us.

Have you done something that You haven't confessed to God? Why not do it now?

Dear heavenly Father, thank You for not allowing me to hide behind others. Thank You for the gift of truth and Your love and mercy that will always free me from sin. In Jesus' name. Amen.

The Price of Independence

To the woman [the LORD God] said, "I will greatly increase your
pains in childbearing; with pain you will give birth to children.
Your desire will be for your husband, and he will rule over you."

GENESIS 3:16

Only a parent can understand how God feels when we choose our
own way over His. Only a parent can understand how God grieves
when we make wrong choices. Perhaps the punishment for Eve was so she
would feel what God felt in the moment she decided to become her own
god. And, even worse, how God feels when we choose to love something
more than Him.

Genesis 3:16 has been wrongfully tagged as a support for a wife's submission to her husband, but that's not it at all. If that were true, the curse would
have applied to married women only. No, this declaration was a universal
observance of what would rule a woman's heart if God weren't seated on the
throne of her heart. This is something *all* women can relate to.

Eve's desire for her husband would rule her. This may explain why single
women are sometimes consumed with the search for a perfect mate to "complete" them. The frustration of realizing no human can do that—only God—is
often not discovered by most until after they're married. Until then the fan-
tasy does its work of tormenting those who long to feel completed and be
validated by a spouse.

Only God can fill the void in our hearts. Hopefully this understanding will
help us understand and allow people to be who they are—imperfect humans.
Turn to God and look to Him for fulfillment, security, and happiness.

How does your desire for a mate rule you? Your decisions? Your habits?

---

*Dear heavenly Father, I pray that I will look to You...and only
You...for everything. In Jesus' name. Amen.*

The Chaos of Wrong Choices

To Adam [the LORD God] said, "Because you listened to your wife and ate from the tree about which I commanded you, 'You must not eat of it,' Cursed is the ground because of you; through painful toil you will eat of it all the days of your life. It will produce thorns and thistles for you…By the sweat of your brow you will eat your food until you return to the ground, since from it you were taken."

GENESIS 3:17-19

*H*ere is where the great divide occurred between man and woman. For the woman her sense of identity would be wrapped up in her husband and children. Both of these areas close to her heart would prove difficult to navigate and be a constant source of angst outside of the grace of God. The man would find his identity in his work, in his ability to be fruitful and productive. He would define himself by his accomplishments. In a sense God said to the man, "Okay, you want to be independent? Run everything by yourself without My help!" And because the man is not God, nature resists his efforts, making things difficult. Notice that Adam wasn't just chastised and corrected for eating the fruit. He was also in trouble because he listened to Eve instead of obeying God.

The chaos that followed that afternoon snack in the garden continues. Men and women find themselves at odds even though they long for the same thing. The fruit divided Adam and Eve and compromised their ability to relate to one another. They would have to fight to maintain their relationship for the rest of their lives. They no longer would truly understand one another.

No matter how much we love people, we must never allow them to lead us beyond the voice of God!

What influences have caused you to ignore God's instructions? What was the outcome?

———————————— ❖ ————————————

Dear heavenly Father, forgive me for the times other voices drown out Yours in my life. In Jesus' name. Amen.

The Fight for Identity

Adam named his wife Eve, because she would
become the mother of all the living.
GENESIS 3:20

*A*dam's last official duty before he and his wife were banished from Eden was to give her a new name. He originally called her "Woman," identifying with their oneness. But Eve's act of independence separated her from Adam. She now had her own identity. She was still his wife, but she would also become the mother of all living things.

Most single women spend their time seeking their soul mates. But after marriage, the wife begins to fight to maintain her own identity. This flies in the face of the "oneness" God prescribed for the marital union as an earthly reflection of our oneness with Him. Two becoming one means there is a blending of two lives, a surrender of two wills for the betterment of the whole.

If we are truly dead to the flesh and alive in Christ, our identity is hidden in Him. He will give us all new names when we see Him. He will restore us to complete oneness with Him. Until then we struggle with our independent nature while searching for a man to give us a "name," to validate us. It's a vicious cycle that can end at the foot of the cross when we gladly allow Christ to give us new identities—that of being new creatures who no longer insist on our own way. When we allow Christ to name us, whether we have husbands or not, our identity remains secure.

The struggle to establish who we are, why we are here, and what we are to do is not with a man or anyone else. These questions are answered when we discover who we are in Christ—and rest in that knowledge.

In what ways do you struggle with your identity? What would it take to settle this for you?

———————————— ✠ ————————————

Heavenly Father, I delight in the name You've given me—beloved. Help me to rest in who I am in You. In Jesus' name. Amen.

The Covering of God

The LORD God made garments of skin
for Adam and his wife and clothed them.
GENESIS 3:21

*I*n our nakedness He clothes us
In our despair he quiets us
In our brokenness He binds our wounds and heals us
In our hunger He fills us
He quenches our thirst to be filled
Washed
Restored
And when we feel we have nowhere to turn
He gently leads us forward
Who told you that you were naked?
Who told you that you would never be loved the
way you long to be?
Who told you that you would never find the fulfillment
you seek?
'Tis the enemy
Whispering in the darkness of night
Look to the light
See Him waiting for you to run into His arms
Allow Him to embrace and cover you
Cover your nakedness
And warm you with His love

What do you need today?

———————————— ⸭ ————————————

*Dear heavenly Father, I stand before You in need of one thing—
You! In Jesus' name. Amen.*

Intimacy Restored

Adam lay with his wife Eve, and she became
pregnant and gave birth to Cain.

GENESIS 4:1

*T*oday's verse is one of the most profound to me. Adam lay with his wife. Sexual intimacy occurred. We know nothing of Adam and Eve's relationship in Eden past the initial discovery, celebration, naming, and subsequent fall of them both. But now they're out in the world, and the first thing mentioned is their coming together in this miraculous way. Their bond is solidified and reestablished by this very personal act that results in Cain being conceived. Cain is born, a child of the flesh who walks in the flesh throughout his life.

Our first attempts will always be born of the flesh. It is only when we seek to know and please God that we bear the fruit of the Spirit and carry the attributes of Christ to the world.

God already knows us. We are the ones who must seek to know Him beyond face value. In knowing Him and worshiping Him, His seed is planted in our spirits, and we become pregnant with His kingdom's purpose. The word "worship" suggests a place of intimacy with the Lover of our souls, a place where we are filled with Him and all that He is to the point of unspeakable joy. This is true fulfillment. And in Him we find the love and peace we've been looking for.

There is a place of exchange in our relationships that bears fruit. This should be the goal of every interaction. To press past the surface conversations we have and plant God's seeds of love that offer life to those we encounter.

How is your love life with God? What do you know about Him?

Dear heavenly Father, I want to know You the way You know me—deeply and intimately. In Jesus' name. Amen.

The Gift of Fruitfulness

[Eve] said, "With the help of the LORD I have brought forth a man."
GENESIS 4:1

A friend just wrote me a note saying "Grace wounds before it heals." How true. God sometimes allows us to experience pain so we'll see our need for Him. Eve's little trek with independence brought her back to the place of realizing how much she needed the God she momentarily shunned. Now the pain of birthing a child reminded her of her limited strength. She acknowledges, "With the help of the Lord I have brought forth a man."

As we come full circle back into the arms of God after laboring to produce things on our own, we find ourselves at the same wonderful place—secure in God's love.

No matter where we go or what we accomplish, life will always be easier if we joyfully accept God's participation. There is labor, and there is travail. In His original design I don't think He wanted us to experience either. However, through sin it has come to this. And in the midst of our straining to cross the finish line, what we're made of becomes clear. We are nothing without God. It is not by our might, not by our power, but only by God's Spirit that we can accomplish what He sets before us. Anything we bring forth must be championed by Him to truly succeed. "Unless the LORD builds the house, its builders labor in vain" (Psalm 127:1).

What does that mean for us? In our search for love, for accomplishment, for fulfillment, for whatever we desire, God must be a participant in our efforts. Without Him all plans fail, abort, or wither. With Him alone there is life.

What have you tried to accomplish on your own?

Dear heavenly Father, I've tried to do things in my own strength long enough. As I submit to You, please strengthen me by Your Spirit so I will bear Your fruit in all areas of my life. In Jesus' name. Amen.

The key to having successful relationships is first having a successful relationship with God. In our times of intimacy and communion with Him, we learn how to love. As we learn to love Him, we are given the ability to love others on a deeper level. We can then honor, submit, serve, and give ourselves to one another without reserve or inhibition.

But if giving ourselves to God isn't mastered, we will struggle with every earthly relationship we have. We will be bent on seeking only what we can get. Therefore, we will never get enough from anyone. We will become desperate, seeking any and all things that promise the validation and affirmation we feel we need. We'll become more self-absorbed as we search for these core needs in all the wrong places. Only in embracing God's love for us and discovering how to offer our hearts in worship to Him will we be filled with all we need. Then we become whole in Him.

The Cost of True Worship

Abel brought fat portions from some of the firstborn of his flock.
The LORD looked with favor on Abel and his offering, but on
Cain and his offering he did not look with favor. So Cain
was very angry, and his face was downcast.

GENESIS 4:4-5

So often we want what we want from God but are unwilling to give Him what He wants. Abel's offering pleased God, but Cain's didn't. Instead of seeking what would please God, Cain became angry.

I also think of Aaron's sons Nadab and Abihu, who offered an unauthorized fire offering to the Lord. Perhaps they mixed up their own incense concoction even though God had provided a recipe. Or maybe they didn't do the offering at the right time. We're not given the exact nature of the offense, just that God wasn't pleased by their independence. When they lit their incense, it flared, and the fire consumed them.

Perhaps we're no longer mixing incense, but we are certainly making decisions on how much worship we're willing to give to God and what we're willing to do. We tend to want to be just obedient enough to keep our agendas intact. And when God resists our selfishness and willfulness by refusing to bless our efforts, we are consumed with disappointment, with despair over our unanswered prayers, with questions asking why God hasn't appeared on the scene, with anger because our sense of entitlement hasn't been met.

Hope deferred makes the heart sick, but how justifiable is that when we have disappointed God? When we've put our own desires ahead of His? We need to put ourselves back under God's authority and direction and instructions before He will fully bless us with the desires of our hearts.

Do you feel God is withholding something from you? What is it? How do you feel about the situation?

———————————— ❖ ————————————

Dear heavenly Father, forgive me for my attitude. I long to offer worship that will please You. I'll start by sacrificing my agendas so You can have Your way. Amen.

Attitude Adjustments

Then the LORD said to Cain, "Why are you angry? Why is your face
downcast? If you do what is right, will you not be accepted?
But if you do not do what is right, sin is crouching at your door;
it desires to have you, but you must master it."

GENESIS 4:6

Attitude is key. If we're disappointed or angry with God, no good
will come from it. The more we rehearse what He hasn't done for
us and why we're "entitled" to what we want, the deeper into the quicksand of bitterness we will go. Our hearts will become hard, and the distance
between God and us will widen, unnoticed by us, until we find ourselves
in a wasteland of self-destruction.

The solution to crossing the chasm between our disappointment and God's
way almost seems too simple. All we have to do is "Do the right thing." We
begin by changing our attitude. Anger is deceptive because it makes us feel
we are stronger than we really are. Anger comes from feeling our rights have
been violated. "God owes me this" is what anger screams. "I'm justified in
digging in my heels and refusing to praise Him or cooperate with His will,"
we decide. In our anger we forget that God is God and we are not.

Thankfully, God understands our human tendency to anger, and He gives
us permission to be angry as long as it doesn't lead to sin. Healthy anger is
expressed in a gentle manner and diffused before the sun goes down. Anger
that goes unbridled is dangerous. It raises its puny fist at God and demands
what it isn't entitled to. And God will not be dictated to. Without retaliation
or force, He advises us that we need to master our attitude to avoid becoming a slave to sin. Either we will master sin or sin will master us.

What are you insisting on? What is your attitude when you don't get
your way?

---

*Dear heavenly Father, I realize that my will is involved in my
attitude. I choose to release anger and disappointment and
embrace hope in You. Help me release all that has bound me.
In Jesus' name. Amen.*

The Treachery of Insecurity

And while they were in the field,
Cain attacked his brother Abel and killed him.

Genesis 4:8

When we don't resolve our issues with God, someone will get hurt. An issue about acceptable offerings that was between Cain and God mushroomed into an entirely unexpected end. Cain killed his brother. He decided to eliminate what he thought was standing between him and a blessing instead of dealing with the real cause—himself. How often do we do that?

Our insecurity causes us to hurt someone else's feelings through sarcasm, insult, or action. We're insensitive to the needs of another because we're too steeped in our own pain. We magnify and personalize little things into imagined offenses and strike out, at times harming people who had nothing to do with our core issues.

We may not be killing people physically, but we maim them. With our attitudes, a glance, a word, we can inflict deep wounds that we often fail to see. We leave people bleeding in our wakes. And all the while God is observing how we're handling situations. It grieves Him when we don't control our wills by asking for His help and submitting to Him. A life under the Spirit of God doesn't do anything to grieve the heart of God. A life under God thrives and manifests His love to others.

What negative attitudes have you allowed to go unchecked? What areas of your life do you need to submit to God?

Dear heavenly Father, I long to be a vessel that only gives life. Put to death anything in me that hinders me in serving and representing You. In Jesus' name. Amen.

Brotherly Obligation

Then the LORD said to Cain, "Where is your brother Abel?"
"I don't know," he replied. "Am I my brother's keeper?"
GENESIS 4:9

The concept of being responsible for someone other than yourself can feel foreign to someone who walks alone. Independence can be as much a curse as it is a blessing. "In-dependent." The very structure of the word encourages us to go within ourselves. To depend on no one but ourselves. Not God. Not a man, a friend, or a family member. No one. And we can master being self-sufficient to a great degree. However, the more time we take to serve ourselves, the less time we have to serve others. This is a very common malady among singles. Our lives can become myopic, rendering us less sensitive to others.

Are we our brother or sister's keeper? Indeed, we are. As members of the body of Christ, we are called to bear one another's burdens. To mourn with those who weep and celebrate with those who rejoice. To bear the infirmities of the weak if we are stronger. We are encouraged in Scripture to help others if we have something they need rather than just saying, "I will be praying for you." God says that what we do for the least of people we do for Him. When we care for the less fortunate, we become His hands reaching out to those He wants to touch and bless. In this way we are all accountable for how we treat each other. Life isn't just for the sake of living. It's also for the sake of imparting God's love.

Who is God calling you to touch today?

———————————— ✖ ————————————

Dear heavenly Father, make me an instrument of Your care to others today. In Jesus' name. Amen.

Godly Reflections

When God created man, he made him in the likeness of God.
GENESIS 5:1

The first thing God said about mankind was "Let us make man in our image, in our likeness." We were created to not only reflect God's power and love, but also to represent Him on the earth. We're to imitate Christ and manifest the fruit of the Holy Spirit.

Are you wondering, *What does God look like?* We are called to imitate God in His character and attributes. And we can know what those are by reading His Word and talking to Him. As we walk in daily interaction with the Holy Spirit, He reveals the heart and the character of God the Father and God the Son. This provides a road map on how to live this life and accomplish God's desires.

Jesus was God on earth. He didn't live according to His own agenda. Maybe He wanted to get married and have children. Maybe He wanted to do something other than heal the sick and preach the good news. Perhaps some people got on His nerves, and He wondered why He volunteered to die for them. And yet He said, "I love the Father and...do exactly what my Father has commanded me" (John 14:31). Jesus came to reconcile us to God and bring us back into intimate relationship with Him.

We are called to do the same (as much as possible in our humanity). We're to put aside our personal agendas in order to glorify God and reveal the heart of God to those who may not know Him. The wonderful surprise is that as we strive to fulfill God's desire, our own desires are met! Jesus laid down His life because it was the desire of the Father, but in the exchange He gained His desire—a beautiful bride, which is the church...us! Oh, how much we will gain as we purpose to be like Him...to become like Him.

What is keeping you from imitating Christ?

───────────── ✠ ─────────────

*Dear heavenly Father, help me be more like You every day.
In Jesus' name. Amen.*

The Reflection of Influence

When Adam had lived 130 years, he had a son in his
own likeness, in his own image; and he named him Seth.

GENESIS 5:3

*W*e have the ability to duplicate ourselves. In a sense, that's what happens as part of my ministry. As I travel I'm always amazed when women approach me with stories about how their lives were changed by something they read in one of my books or heard in a message I shared. Even more amazing is the women who share with me that my words have influenced their decision-making process.

Some time ago "What would Jesus do?" became a catchphrase that called us to go against our natural inclinations and imitate Christ in every situation. As we did this, we became examples for others to follow. As we strive to be more like Jesus—creative, productive, holy, loving, and gracious, our lives should become contagious to others. As a single woman, the ability to bear offspring is not limited to having children. Our lives can impact those around us by enticing them to want what we have. To serve whom we serve. Based on what we reflect, people may follow our example and choose, in essence, to look like us. The mission for us is to be more like Jesus so others will see Him and desire Him. Can you imagine an earth filled with Jesus' glory? Wouldn't that be exciting? Oh, to be more like Christ! But better still—to cause others to see Him and choose to accept Him as Lord and Savior!

In what ways are you duplicating Christ in your social circle?

———————————— ✠ ————————————

*Dear heavenly Father, help me be a living example of Your
Son, Jesus. In His name I pray. Amen.*

Walking with God

Enoch walked with God; then he was no more,
because God took him away.
GENESIS 5:24

irds of a feather flock together. The concept that we become like the people we hang out with has been proven time and time again. In Ghana, West Africa, when a couple is courting, they say they are "walking together." Have you ever noticed that when married couples have been together for a while they begin to look alike? This is the epitome of becoming one. They get to the place where they can finish each other's sentences and anticipate each other's desires.

Something happens when we walk with God. The exchange between us becomes more and more intimate. We come to a place of divine intimacy, where we lose more and more of ourselves and take on more and more of His traits and heart. If we truly want to get to the place where we echo the sentiments of Paul and declare, "It is no longer I who live, but Christ lives in me," we must be willing to take the time to press into the heart of God.

Have you ever had such a great conversation with someone that it was hard to end the exchange? I can only imagine the conversation that day between Enoch and God on the day God took him to heaven. Whatever they were talking about, obviously neither one wanted their time together to end. I'm sure that this man who sought God and prophesied to his neighbors left a lasting impression with all whom he encountered. Perhaps after he departed many people chose to walk the same trail, seeking God for themselves.

What is your alone time with God like?

Dear heavenly Father, I want to be one with You. Draw me closer to You so I can know You more intimately. In Jesus' name. Amen.

The Exception

But Noah found favor in the eyes of the Lord.
GENESIS 6:8

*N*oah lived in a time when, very much like today, everyone pretty much did what they pleased. Mankind was into the pursuit of pleasure and all that fed the flesh. There was little concern about pursuing godly things or pleasing a holy God. In the midst of this anything-goes atmosphere was a man quietly living by faith. He watched a generation caught up in greed, lust, lasciviousness, dishonesty, and, well...you know all the things we're witnessing right now. Noah, like most of us, shook his head in sad concern, pondering when God would do something.

Sometimes it's hard to shake the feeling that those around us are doing whatever they please and getting away with it. Where is the reward in being righteous and doing things God's way? Aren't there times when you feel like the lone voice of reason crying in the wilderness? Do you wonder every once in a while if you're sticking to God's standards for nothing? Has a little voice in the back of your mind whispered, "Perhaps holiness is not that important. Why be celibate? Why try to live holy?" And then the answer comes...

Noah found favor in the eyes of the Lord. And God was moved once again to separate the darkness from the light. Instructing Noah to build an ark, He warned him of impending rain. He promised to preserve Noah and his family while the rest of the sinful world perished. Noah's faith and life of righteousness was rewarded. Year after year he worked on the ark, even though it had never rained before. His faith motivated him to steadfastly obey God when there was no evidence that his obedience would pay off. And then the rain began. And righteousness had its last say.

What areas of living a holy life do you struggle with?

———————————— ————————————

Dear heavenly Father, please give me the strength it takes to continue walking in holiness. Let me find favor in Your sight. In Jesus' name. Amen.

The Robbery of Entitlement

The LORD then said to Noah, "Go into the ark, you and your whole
family, because I have found you righteous in this generation."
GENESIS 7:1

The greatest reward for righteousness is that we're covered and protected by God. He remains faithful to those who are faithful to Him. But sometimes it's easy for us to fall into the trap of believing that God owes us something in return for our obedience. We look at our works of righteousness as bargaining tools to get what we want from God. Many people see life this way and struggle with being angry at God when their demands are met with silence.

God owes us nothing. He has already given us everything, including a way of escape from sin and corruption through His Son, Jesus Christ. Our obedience is our thank-you to Him for restoring our ability to have an intimate relationship with Him. If we lose sight of this fact or it escapes our minds, it's easy to drop into bartering with God. "God, I'll be celibate if you'll send a mate quickly." "I'll increase my tithe if You get me a better job." "I'll be obedient to You for a sign that lets me know You see what I do."

On days when discouragement hits and you're tempted by what others have or the life they lead, talk to God about it! He understands. Ask Him to open your eyes to the blessings He's given you. And then why not make an actual list of how God has worked in your life?

The day will come when we will look back and see what we've been saved from as we rest in the shadow of God's wings.

Have you tried to bargain with God? What was the result? How do you keep from doing that now?

*Heavenly Father, I surrender my all to You. I choose to rest
in the safety You provide when I obey You. In Jesus' name.
Amen.*

*A Life
of Promise*

Single or not, God has given every human vast promise. The process of becoming can be a painful one, with many detours away from our dreams. Whether we dream of mates, being swept off our feet by knights in shining armor, climbing up the corporate ladder, or achieving fame and fortune, there will be a time of preparation, of stripping, of breaking, of rebuilding from the inside out. In order to receive the perfect blessings, we must be willing to be perfected. God doesn't just want to bless us. He wants us to be able to maintain and sustain the blessings He bestows. As He molds and prepares us for His purposes, we need to trust His heart when we can't see His hand at work. Yes, we must learn to wait on the Lord, no matter what.

The Way of Favor

Now Israel loved Joseph more than any of his other sons,
because he had been born to him in his old age;
and he made a richly ornamented robe for him.

GENESIS 37:3

Joseph was a son after the heart of his father. Joseph nurtured his relationship with his dad. He spent time with Israel, carrying out his every request. He had a genuine love free from the feelings of entitlement his other brothers had toward their father. The brothers had many "daddy issues" based on the "mama drama" they witnessed as their mother and Joseph's mother vied for their husband's love. Their mothers' pain became their pain, turning to anger in some and rebellion in others. They felt Israel owed them something.

Israel lavished love on Joseph. He may have been considered a spoiled brat, a Goody Two-shoes, but that didn't seem to faze Joseph. He loved his father. And his father loved him back, giving him a very special token that spoke volumes about how he felt. The coat signified his favor and announced it to the world.

In Israel's relationship with his sons I see a counterpoint in our relationships with God. God says He loves those who love Him and punishes those who hate Him and do evil (Deuteronomy 7:9-10). Our attitudes affect God's responses to us. Our love for Him makes us joyfully obedient to Him. In return, He dresses us with His favor and His delight.

I'm sure Israel loved all his sons. But some were easier to love than others because of their attitudes. "God does not show favoritism" in that He accepts people from every nation who choose to come to Him. However, I believe He does favor people based on where they place Him in their hearts.

What is your attitude toward your heavenly Father? Is God first in your life?

---

*Dear heavenly Father, may Your face shine upon me and grant
me favor as I honor You with my love and praise. Amen.*

The Distortion of Envy

When his brothers saw that their father loved [Joseph]
more than any of them, they hated him
and could not speak a kind word to him.
GENESIS 37:4

*Y*ou will be hated by all nations because of me," Jesus said. God's favor doesn't necessarily gain us a fan club, especially because we have what others want. Let's look beyond the fault of hate and see what people need. Purpose to be sensitive. Perhaps our celebration of the favor we receive from God can be tempered in the presence of those who aren't faring so well.

Even as Christians we fall short of God's standards of rejoicing with others. I know I've caught myself just before spitting out venom concerning this person or that one. I praise the Lord that I was stopped short by the Holy Spirit, who pointed out my envy and jealousy.

Envy can distort our attitudes and affect our character if we allow it to go unchecked. Whether we're always a bridesmaid and never a bride or chafing as we watch someone not as qualified as us receive a promotion, the temptation remains the same. We want to deride the one who has gained what we want and cite all the reasons she shouldn't have it.

Perhaps we need to examine what she did to get what we wanted. Or maybe we need an attitude adjustment. If Joseph's brothers had shown a better attitude, would they have eventually received their own elaborately fashioned coats from their father? Who knows? But as long as the focus was on Joseph, they couldn't correct or change their own behavior. And so it is with us. Our ability to gain what we want in life begins with us.

Who have you envied in the past? What did you feel was lacking in your life?

---- ✢ ----

Heavenly Father, let me always begin with You when searching for information or answers. Search my heart and show me the hidden things I need to address. In Jesus' name. Amen.

A Test of Faith

Joseph had a dream, and when he told it to
his brothers, they hated him all the more.
GENESIS 37:5

Special dreams can be difficult. Joseph's dreams got him into big trouble with his brothers. *How dare you have a dream like that!* they thought when Joseph told them his vision. *Who are you to dream of such a thing?* Dreams are birthed in the bosom of our heavenly Father. When we draw close to Him and worship and honor Him, He shares what He's been planning.

Dreams are fragile, so guard them closely. Pray and wait. Sometimes they are not to be shared at their inception. This is when they can be put down or even sabotaged by those who seek to kill in others what they don't have themselves. Be careful who you share your dreams with!

Lest you get too excited, know that dreams invite tests—tests of your relationships, your faith, your attitudes, and your character. And dreams are just the beginning of a potential shift in your life.

What dreams are you harboring in your heart? How has your faith been tried by what you envisioned?

Dear heavenly Father, thank You for sharing Your heart with me. Help me to stand in faith even when I am confronted with opposition. In Jesus' name. Amen.

The Root of Envy

But [Joseph's brothers] saw him in the distance,
and before he reached them, they plotted to kill him.
GENESIS 37:18

*T*rust me, when you have something deposited in your spirit by God, others will see you coming. You don't need to proclaim God is with you, announce who you are, or describe how important you are. You don't have to have a "don't you know who I am and who you are dealing with" attitude. It's clear to others what may not even be that clear to you. There is something different when the anointing of God rests on you. It goes before you, declaring that someone special just entered the room. A force to be reckoned with has arrived.

I remember when I was in school there was a very pretty girl in my class who didn't really know she was pretty. All the other girls envied her beauty. The facts that she was well liked by the boys and nice didn't help either. What was just part of who she was made her peers despise her. "She thinks she's cute," they muttered. Well, the fact of the matter was *they* thought she was cute. She didn't give it a second thought.

Her foes sought to kill her. Not literally...just in her spirit. They glared at her, snubbed her, and were most unkind, which made her very sad. Her days at school were difficult. But each day she would return with the same smile on her face, being nice in spite of their horridness. I wonder if she had a mother who had the discernment to tell her to overlook the jealousy of her schoolmates and pity them instead of becoming a victim. And indeed, she was a victor, leaving them to their own devices until they grew weary of not winning.

Some people try to destroy what they can't attain. Don't let them.

Have you felt criticized and despised by people? What were they trying to destroy in you? How did you rise above their doubts and criticism?

Dear heavenly Father, when doubts assault my dreams, and the attitudes of others threaten to harm what You've placed in me, preserve me. In Jesus' name. Amen.

Dare to Dream

"Here comes that dreamer!" they said to each other.
GENESIS 37:19

Someone asked me the other day what legacy Martin Luther King left me. My answer was immediate: "The knowledge of the power of a dream." I'm sure there were many who thought him a dreamer. And surely some people sought to kill him. But the beauty of a dream is that it often lives on long after the dreamer is gone. This is when we realize the dream was bigger than the dreamer.

"God dreams" can be overwhelming. Have you ever had a God dream? You know it's a dream from Him when the desire in the dream seems greater than your ability to make it happen. Take heart! He delights in bringing the seemingly impossible to pass.

Working with famous music producer Michael Omartian, Christian author Stormie Omartian's husband, was something I wrote on my wish list many, many years ago. Twenty-eight years ago, to be exact. Time passed, and though I met him, I never brought up my dream or thought more about it. Fast forward to 2007. There I was, in Michael's studio leaning against his baby grand piano, recording a song I wrote. In the middle of the project I felt like God tapped me on the shoulder and said, "I remembered!" I wept. It was true. I had long surrendered my little wish, but at the appointed time God moved and brought it to pass.

People may think what you long for is foolish, but God takes our dreams seriously, especially if He plants them in our hearts to begin with. The secret to finding true joy and overcoming frustration is knowing the difference between our wants and God's desires. Dream on!

What secret desires are you harboring in your heart?

Dear heavenly Father, separate my wishes from Your desires, and bring what You propose to life. In Jesus' name. Amen.

The Discomfort of Change

So when Joseph came to his brothers, they stripped him of
his robe—the richly ornamented robe he was wearing.

GENESIS 37:23

*L*ife experience teaches us that before we can move to the next level, we must be stripped of something. New wine can't be contained in an old wineskin (it will burst). Even that which is seemingly comfortable has to be stripped away if it isn't conducive to where we're going. And sometimes the things we cling to get in the way of what we truly want.

I always ask singles who express the desire to be married if they're really ready for marriage. Sad but true, many have gotten quite comfortable in the lives they lead, not realizing they've become self-oriented. In almost every case where change is involved, God allows discomfort to move us from where we presently are to where He wants to take us. Sometimes the changes seem cruel and jolting to us, but the results are what matters. God's plans for us are always greater and better than where we presently live and what we are experiencing. It's important to not dwell on the messenger or the offense or the one who initiates the change that we might not be welcoming at the present time. They are mere instruments in the design of where God is taking us. In many cases the people who are closest to us seem to cause us the most hurt, which creates a motivation for change. But God remains faithful in spite of the humanity of those around us.

With this knowledge we have a choice. We can cling to what will have to go anyway or joyfully surrender it and move on. Here's to onward and upward!

What things, habits, or mindsets are you clinging to that might be delaying a blessing from God?

———————————— ✠ ————————————

Dear heavenly Father, help me let go of everything that hinders me from receiving what You have for me. In Jesus' name. Amen.

The Path Toward Your Dream

So when the Midianite merchants came by, his brothers pulled
Joseph up out of the cistern and sold him for twenty shekels
of silver to the Ishmaelites, who took him to Egypt.

GENESIS 37:28

When sudden changes in life occur, don't despair. Sometimes we have to go where we don't want to in order to get what we want. At times it may seem we're being taken even further away from the desire of our hearts, but God knows the plans He has for us and He'll bring them about.

Moses wanted to save his people, but the prerequisite was spending 40 years on the back side of the desert. David was appointed king, but he spent years hiding from King Saul in the wilderness. All of this was for the sake of their character development. You see, we must be ready to receive the dream...sustain the dream...keep the dream intact.

Often we're so excited about the prospect of the dream that we don't take the time to think of the groundwork that must be laid or the responsibilities the dream will bring to bear. But God does! And so for a season He sets us apart to prepare us for what is to come.

At times like these we can listen to the enemy and settle into low self-esteem, devaluing all that God has done in our lives and losing hope for the future. But now is not the time to listen to the lies of Satan! Instead, remain steadfast in God. Seek Him and don't despise the process of preparation. You will come forth from God's purifying fire as pure gold.

What is the value of your dream? Where are you willing to go? What are you willing to endure to get what you want from God?

Dear heavenly Father, help me trust Your heart even when I can't see Your hand at work. In Jesus' name. Amen.

The Gift Within

Now Joseph had been taken down to Egypt. Potiphar, an
Egyptian who was one of Pharaoh's officials, the captain of the
guard, bought him from the Ishmaelites who had taken him there.

GENESIS 39:1

Sometimes the world can see what those closest to us can't. This is part of God's glorious plan to place us in position for blessing. He is not opposed to moving us in whatever manner He needs to. Sometimes getting fired or rejected has nothing to do with what we thought it did. Things are not always what they appear. Geography can play a major part in our blessing, so God might need to get us to move.

Many Christians chafe at serving bosses who are not believers, and yet this is often where God does His finest work with us. As we reflect His character in the secular marketplace, the light of God shines brightly and shatters the darkness. As we uphold godly standards to those who surround us, we display our love for God, and He draws those we encounter to Him.

Sometimes the world doesn't even know why it's attracted to us. There is just something about us. That "something" is called an "anointing." A sweetness that comes from dwelling with God and allowing Him to break us in order to make us who He wants us to be—people who glorify Him and share His love with others.

We've been bought for a price by Jesus' death to accomplish one thing—the purpose of God. Joseph, a man who was single and walked alone, was set apart to do great things for God. Perhaps at this point in your life you find yourself in a place you don't want to be. Do you feel isolated or wronged? I encourage you to have hope because you and I know God is up to something that will be revealed in His timing.

Where are you now? Are you feeling out of place or misplaced? Where do you think you should be?

———————————— ✠ ————————————

Dear heavenly Father, forgive me for despairing over my place
in life. Help me to rest in the knowledge that You have a plan.
In Jesus' name. Amen.

The Faithfulness of God

The LORD was with Joseph and he prospered,
and he lived in the house of his Egyptian master.
GENESIS 39:2

*W*e can be blessed in the strangest places if we're open to the fact that God is not limited by where we are or our circumstances. Even slavery can free other things within us…if we submit to the process. I truly believe that when God doesn't get us out of where we are, it's because He is refining us or using us to influence other people. Contrary to popular belief, God *does* allow us to go through difficult circumstances for periods of time so He can finish the work of transformation.

He will allow others to be in authority over us, even if they believe everything contrary to our core values, and still bless us in that place. This is how God glorifies Himself. The Egyptians were sold on their gods. And they had hundreds of them, one for anything and everything you can imagine. Joseph had only one. I'm sure those around Joseph were in a state of dismay. How could this Israelite slave, the lowest of the low, prosper in favor and promotion? Because of the God he served! A God they didn't know.

Joseph may have gone down to a place of low estate, but the Lord was still with Him. And the Lord is also with you where you are. He will nurture, sustain, and bless you in your situation. Look for Him in the midst of the trial and acknowledge His presence.

What or who is ruling over you right now? What circumstances do you feel you can't change but would like to?

Dear heavenly Father, help me to not despise the process of becoming. Let me sense Your presence more than before in the midst of my struggles. In Jesus' name. Amen.

The Keeping Power of God

When his master saw that the LORD was with [Joseph] and that the LORD gave him success in everything he did, Joseph found favor in his eyes and became his attendant. Potiphar put him in charge of his household, and he entrusted to his care everything he owned.

GENESIS 39:3

The world is looking for living examples of Christ, and the presence of God should be so evident in our lives that others take notice. So how are we conducting ourselves in our day-to-day interactions? Is there a difference between us and those we work with (if they aren't believers)? When the others are lamenting about a man shortage or other difficulties in life, do we chime in with our own complaints? Or are we exhibiting a peace about these circumstances that they can't fathom?

We are *in* the world but not *of* the world (John 15:19). Like Joseph, we live in an environment that is foreign to us. We have pledged allegiance to a different kingdom—God's kingdom—and it should show. This doesn't mean we walk around with long faces trying to look super spiritual, but there should be a difference in the way we deal with the situations that are common to everyone. We should model a peace that passes understanding and a joy in the midst of uncertainty that can only come from God. These make up the unexplainable excellence in our lives that others want.

Our responses to life and all that it throws at us gets the attention of those we encounter. A tree doesn't pick where it is planted; it grows anyway. As we respond positively to God walking with us through the difficult places, He showers us with favor.

In what ways have you experienced God's peace in difficult circumstances?

———————————— ✠ ————————————

Dear heavenly Father, help me remember who I really serve—You! In Jesus' name. Amen.

The Favor of God

From the time [Potiphar] put [Joseph] in charge of his household
and of all that he owned, the LORD blessed the household of the
Egyptian because of Joseph. The blessing of the LORD was on
everything Potiphar had, both in the house and in the field.

GENESIS 39:5

If you've found yourself in a situation where you feel that those who care nothing for God seem to have way more than you, look again. Perhaps they are being blessed for your sake. I remember working for a boss many years ago who was not a nice man. He was very wealthy and wasn't paying what I felt I deserved for the job I was doing. He gave me a hard time and was very coarse with his language. Finally one day in frustration I put my hand on my hip and looked him squarely in the eyes. I told him I would no longer tolerate him talking to me the way he did. And just in case he wasn't aware, he was only being blessed because I was working for him. At this he hung his head and said, "I know." Imagine my surprise! He knew God's hand was on my life. The Lord had given me favor to sell everything I worked on to his clients.

After I left his company, his business declined. Sometimes God is blessing others to ensure our provision. Blessings don't always indicate God's approval. God will bless someone so that person can favor one of His children.

We should never compare ourselves to others because we never know the end of the matter. The grass may only appear greener...so take a closer look.

What situation have you been viewing as unfair? Who have you compared yourself to and why?

———————————— ✠ ————————————

Dear heavenly Father, help me stay focused on You. Keep my heart pure so that I won't slip into judgment mode. In Jesus' name. Amen.

The Timing of Temptation

After a while his master's wife took notice of Joseph and said,
"Come to bed with me!" But he refused.
GENESIS 39:7-8

One Bible translation says that Potiphar's wife said to Joseph, "Come lie with me." This is truth on several levels. Intimacy without commitment is a lie. It is based on nothing and holds no promise of tomorrow. This disregards the power of love and sex. It dismisses the awe we should have as we experience this gift from God and walk in reverent fear and respect for one another's bodies that are temples of the Holy Spirit. A casual approach to intimacy doesn't comprehend that sex is a physical parallel to the spiritual act of worship. It's giving all we have and all we are to the mates we've committed to through God. Physical intimacy is not something to participate in lightly.

When the favor of God is on our lives, we will always be noticed. And like Jospeh's situation, it's sometimes by the wrong people for the wrong reasons. This is why we should decide ahead of time what we'll stand up for, what we won't give in to, and what we're willing to negotiate. Temptation seems to come at our lowest points, when we're discouraged, angry, or upset. It often comes when we've been waiting on God to deliver on a promise. It sometimes comes whispering, "You owe it to yourself. You deserve it," pulling at your resistance and your flesh.

In spite of how we feel, when we stay submitted to God, He will reward our faithfulness.

What tempts you when you're struggling? What can you do to stay strong?

Dear heavenly Father, help me stand firm when I grow weary and question Your faithfulness. Thank You for establishing my commitment to You and Your commitment to me on a firm foundation—Jesus Christ. In His name I pray. Amen.

Finding the Power to Stand

"How then could I do such a wicked thing and sin against God?"
And though she spoke to Joseph day after day, he refused to
go to bed with her or even be with her.

GENESIS 39:9-10

Staying focused on why you have chosen holiness is critical to remaining holy. What blesses me the most about Joseph's response to Potiphar's wife is that his focus wasn't on what would happen if he sinned, on what the consequences would be. No, his response was totally focused on the heart of God. In spite of all that he had gone through, Joseph cared how God would feel about his actions! He was clear on the fact that even if no one was "hurt," God would be grieved by the sin. I believe that fear of an outcome will never be enough to keep us in line with God. Jesus clearly stated, "If you love me, you will obey what I command" (John 14:15). That should be motivation enough.

When temptation beckons, what is our first thought usually? The fear of being caught, unfortunately. But, if we truly love Him—and as our love grows—the heart of God becomes our primary concern.

Just because you love God doesn't mean you won't be tempted. In fact, it's safe to say you will be tempted. I believe Joseph was tempted. He was also honest with himself about his weaknesses and set boundaries to safeguard his commitment to God. He avoided his master's wife as much as possible. In the fight to stay holy, we must know ourselves, acknowledge our inclinations, and set boundaries to ensure our obedience to God.

What is your response to temptation? What boundaries can you set to protect yourself?

Dear heavenly Father, keep me safe when I can't do it. My first desire is to please You. In Jesus' name. Amen.

The Price of Purity

One day [Joseph] went into the house to attend to his duties,
and none of the household servants was inside. [Potiphar's
wife] caught him by his cloak and said, "Come to bed with
me!" But he left his cloak in her hand and ran out of the
house...When his master heard the story his wife told him,
saying, "This is how your slave treated me," he burned with
anger. Joseph's master took him and put him in prison.

GENESIS 39:11-12,19-20

Living God's way, according to His commands and principles, often requires paying a huge price. "Can I stand the heat?" is the question we must ask. We need to be clear on the reward of following Christ so we will have the courage to stand firm in His name. The decision must be made based on where our real treasure lies because that's where our hearts will be.

We need to grow spiritually mature to the point where our top priority is pleasing God regardless of the cost. Many people have gone before us, sacrificing their livelihoods and even their lives for the gospel of Jesus Christ. Like the apostle Paul, we need to reach the conclusion that we are not ashamed of the gospel. And then we need to live it.

To bring this down to a real-life level, if you're dating a man who is pressuring you for physical intimacy, he doesn't understand your commitment to purity or to God. He's not in right standing with God, so he wouldn't be a good life partner for you. Although it may be painful, release him and seek out someone who is truly devoted to Jesus.

What is most important to you—the acceptance of others or God's pleasure? How can you deal with rejection and misunderstanding as you stand for God?

---

*Dear heavenly Father, help me stay focused on what is of true
value, of what pleases You. In Jesus' name. Amen.*

The Holding Place

While Joseph was there in the prison, the LORD was
with him; he showed him kindness and granted him
favor in the eyes of the prison warden.

GENESIS 39:21

*D*oes singleness sometimes feel like a jail to you? God is with you!
He's still covering you with His favor and love. Though single
life may, at times, seem to be "hard time" for something that's not a crime,
nothing could be further from the truth.

In our alone time God sometimes does His best work in us. He reveals
Himself in sweet ways that we wouldn't experience in any other place or
season of life. So we can treasure this time and place we're in. It is often far
too short-lived and underappreciated until it is over. God has His own way
of getting our attention and setting us apart for Him. How long will we
have to wait before we'll be released? As long as it takes for Him to finish
what He's begun in us. Then and only then will we move to the next stage
of living and loving. In the end, we'll thank our heavenly Father for all His
refining work. In the meantime, let's study to be good students of what He
is teaching so we can pass this test with flying colors.

In what ways do you feel hindered in your life? What could God be point-
ing out during this time? What test has been difficult for you to pass?

---

*Dear heavenly Father, help me not fight this time of testing and
waiting. Show me the good so I can embrace where I am now.
I want to nurture a grateful heart. In Jesus' name. Amen.*

Taking Life off Hold

After they had been in custody for some time, each of the
two men—the cupbearer and the baker of the king of Egypt,
who were being held in prison—had a dream the same night,
and each dream had a meaning of its own.

GENESIS 40:4-5

Is your life on hold? Does where you are at present seem to have nothing to do with your capacity to dream? Dreams are unhindered by time and space. They can't be confined to any set of conditions. Just because it looks like there is no end to your situation, don't stop dreaming. In fact, encourage your dreams!

In the dark places of our lives often everything else falls away, leaving room for God to plant in our hearts what we couldn't or wouldn't receive before. Sometimes He uses dreams to show us what we can't see when we're awake.

Each dream is unique in accordance with our purposes and destinies. My dream will not be your dream, and your dream will not be mine. Our assignments are different. We need to honor our dreams and the dreams of others because, collectively, our dreams fit into the greater vision God has for His kingdom.

Our dreams are often hints of our assignments from God. Allow Him to whisper to you in the darkness and shed light on the hidden plans of His heart for you.

What dreams has God placed in your heart? What can you be doing while you wait?

———————————— ✣ ————————————

*Dear heavenly Father, make Your dreams mine. In Jesus' name.
Amen.*

Hindrance to Blessing

[Joseph said,] "When all goes well with you, remember me
and show me kindness; mention me to Pharaoh and
get me out of this prison. For I was forcibly carried off
from the land of the Hebrews, and even here I have
done nothing to deserve being put in a dungeon."

Genesis 40:14-15

Who can say what we truly deserve, save God? In the midst of our self-justifying, we confirm that the process God has begun in us has yet to be completed. Every time I decided I was ready for the things I'd been asking God for, I soon discovered I wasn't. Any time our flesh makes a pronouncement of insistence, we can question whether we've "died enough" to self to receive what God has for us. If He gave it to us now, would it consume us?

I also believe that when God allows our blessings to be delayed, it's because He's refining us. Let's allow Him to do His work. We will be better for it. Here's a provocative thought. I heard someone say that the moment Joseph announced he didn't deserve to be in prison he "earned" two more years in his cell. That God was waiting for every ounce of entitlement to be eked from his heart so that He could trust Joseph with the assignment and blessing that awaited. Only when Joseph's rights were surrendered on the altar was he released into the fullness of his God-ordained destiny.

How does this play out in our lives? Perhaps as long as we think we are undeservedly single, and as long as we think it is time to get married, there is still more work to be done in our hearts. God wants us to be so surrendered we will only move at His leading. A heart surrendered to Him keeps us safe.

How surrendered are you to God's timing? How would you live differently if you knew you wouldn't be married for another five years?

Dear heavenly Father, I surrender any feelings and thoughts of entitlement to You. Have Your way with my life. In Jesus' name. Amen.

The Right Perspective

Pharaoh said to Joseph, "I had a dream, and no one can interpret
it. But I have heard it said of you that when you hear a dream you
can interpret it." "I cannot do it," Joseph replied to Pharaoh,
"but God will give Pharaoh the answer he desires."
GENESIS 41:15-16

Trials have a way of putting everything in perspective and reminding us who really is in control. Left to our own devices, we fail miserably time after time. After all is said and done, we discover that no one can figure out our lives better than God. When we've exhausted all other avenues for relief, we go back to God. The key, of course, is to go to God first without going through the trauma of exhausting other resources.

Have you ever had a problem and called your friends—only to discover that not one of them was available to work through the issue with you? Finally you threw up your arms, sat down, got quiet, and waited for God to speak.

God doesn't need to share the credit or glory with anyone else. He is in charge of everything. But before He trusts you with the blessing He has planned, He wants to know if He has your attention and your heart.

What threatens your allegiance to God? How can you keep Him first in your life?

---

*Dear heavenly Father, help me keep my heart grounded in
You. In Jesus' name. Amen.*

When God Decides a Matter

[Joseph said,] "It is just as I said to Pharaoh: God has shown Pharaoh what he is about to do…The reason the dream was given to Pharaoh in two forms is that the matter has been firmly decided by God, and God will do it soon."

Genesis 41:28,32

God will always confirm His Word. What we must do is be still long enough to get clarity on exactly what He is saying to us. Sometimes we get carried off on a whim of our own that ends in a mess. Then the famous question is asked: "What did God speak to you about this situation?" We realize with a sinking feeling that we had dreamed a dream and run off on our own without checking with God.

Our enemy, the devil, loves to give us dreams—to whisper things in our minds that seem good. And sometimes he even sounds like a messenger from God. But be careful. Wait for the confirmation of the Holy Spirit, who will give you confidence and perfect peace if the dream is from God.

The words in today's verses to pay special attention to are "the matter has been firmly decided by God, and God will do it soon." Note it's not what Pharaoh would do. It's what God will do. In our lives, it's not what *we* will do. It's what *God* will do. If we are muscling through to make our dreams happen, manipulating events and individuals, we are deceived. That is not God. That is a dream of our own making.

In what ways has God confirmed your dreams to you?

Dear heavenly Father, grant me the discernment and peace to release the dreams that are not from You. Give me the confidence to hold on to the ones that have been authored by You. In Jesus' name. Amen.

The Power of Surrender

[Joseph said,] "And now let Pharaoh look for a discerning
and wise man and put him in charge of the land of Egypt..."
The plan seemed good to Pharaoh and to all his officials.
So Pharaoh asked them, "Can we find anyone
like this man, one in whom is the spirit of God?"

GENESIS 41:33,37

There have been times in my life when I've met a man, and, even though there was an inkling in the back of my mind that he wasn't "the one," I've forged ahead anyway, happy to finally be getting some male attention. Later I would say to God, when He revealed that my desperation had gotten me into a predicament, "What can You expect? If You put a bone in front of a hungry dog, it's going to go for it!" Now, many years later and much wiser, I'm more reticent and discerning when men approach—no matter how fabulous they appear. I can wait for God's wisdom and signal because I'm finally totally surrendered to God in this area.

I believe Joseph had finally reached that point too. He was so surrendered by the time he stood in front of Pharaoh that he didn't even think of offering his services for a job he knew he was qualified for. This is where God wants all of us. This is when He can trust us to go anywhere. This is when we're ready to receive our hearts' desires. People will also recognize our readiness, and we'll attract the very thing we were chasing.

Has desperation for what you want been repelling the very thing you hope for? What steps can you take to trust God in the situation?

———————————— ✠ ————————————

Dear heavenly Father, help me put my desires to rest so I will be free to receive new ones from You. In Jesus' name. Amen.

The Key to Promotion

Then Pharaoh said to Joseph, "Since God has made
all this known to you, there is no one so discerning and
wise as you. You shall be in charge of my palace, and
all my people are to submit to your orders. Only with
respect to the throne will I be greater than you."

GENESIS 41:39

When God fulfills our hopes and dreams, the results will be greater than we imagined! He is able to do exceedingly, abundantly above all that we can think or imagine. This happens when we are so anchored in our relationships with Him that conversing with Him is second nature. When we are so in tune with His Spirit that we overhear His secrets, it is evident to those around us that we have something they want.

This is when promotion comes. Advancement comes. Whatever you've been hoping and praying for comes. If you move ahead of God's timetable, many lessons will be learned the hard way. When you've spent time with God, the evidence of your relationship with Him will set you apart from others and make entry into promotion possible. Being set apart for God is the gate to a wide thoroughfare of blessing.

What has God been revealing to you lately?

_____ ✸ _____

Dear heavenly Father, please talk to me and guide me. In Jesus' name. Amen.

When Help Matters

Pharaoh gave Joseph the name Zaphenath-Paneah and
gave him Asenath daughter of Potiphera, priest of On, to be
his wife. And Joseph went throughout the land of Egypt.
GENESIS 41:45

God recognizes when we need help. And sometimes our friends or others are the catalysts to completing what God is doing in us. When we get busy about our assignments from God, He will furnish supplies and assistants. He is faithful to give us all that is required when we need it. His timing is impeccable.

I now know I wasn't ready for a mate like I thought I was. And even now I question if I'm ready. If I am to be the "good thing" that God says a wife will be for her husband, I have some issues that need working on in order to not make God a liar. Thankfully, God wants to transform you and me and give us new names in preparation for the work we will do and the alliances we will form for Him. Yes, some of us need more refining than others. As we let God do His work, in the fullness of time everything will fall into place. And all the pieces will fit perfectly! We'll have no questions about which paths we should take. Our dreams—be they mates, careers, or opportunities—will match our assignments and not be a distraction from God's purposes for us. All will be settled and work together for good.

What areas does God still need to work on in you?

———————————— ✠ ————————————

Dear heavenly Father, grant me the patience to allow You to perfect me into a "good thing." In Jesus' name. Amen.

When Joy Comes

Before the years of famine came, two sons were born to Joseph
by Asenath daughter of Potiphera, priest of On. Joseph named his
firstborn Manasseh and said, "It is because God has made me
forget all my trouble and all my father's household."

Genesis 41:50-51

I believe our lives are cyclical. We are either in a good place heading toward a trial, going through a trial, or coming out of a trial. God is faithful to meet us every step of the way, no matter where we are. He gives us what we need to complete the cycle. Whether we're going through or languishing in the desert place with no apparent end in sight, the seasons of our lives are sure to change.

When we're going through a trial, we tend to think we will never get over what's happening. The pain is indelibly stamped in our minds. But like a mother giving birth to a child, though we know intellectually the pain was an undeniable fact, the joy as we look at what we now hold makes the pain pale into a faint memory.

From what we're able to surmise, Joseph suffered being sold into slavery around the time he was 13. He was promoted to the "Pharaoh's right-hand man" position at 30. Do the math. Seventeen years! And yet Joseph states that God has made him forget all he has been through!

What are you struggling with right now that seems as if it will never end? How can you focus your faith on a positive end?

Dear heavenly Father, grant me Your joy in all my trials. In Jesus' name. Amen.

The Value of Trial

The second son [Joseph] named Ephraim and said, "It is because
God has made me fruitful in the land of my suffering."
GENESIS 41:52

Talk about an aha moment! This is when life finally makes sense.
When God gets what He's been working toward in us all along:
fruit. Plain and simple. Suffering should produce fruit—sweet, rich, and
nurturing. Isn't it encouraging to know that the trying of our faith works
patience in us? And when we are patient, God can do His work without
interruption. And we gain valuable experience that creates sound character
in us and makes us more mature in Christ.

People who have suffered major crises have grown much more than those
who have been through only minor problems. There is a graciousness about
them that can't be imitated. We either have it or we don't. Joseph recognized that it was the hand of God that made him what he became. And he
was able to declare the trials were worth it because of what came out of it.
We too will be continually shaped as God prepares us for what He wants
to accomplish through and for us.

In the meantime, let's stick close to the fire and ask God to refine us.

What do you think God is trying to work into your life? What fruit do
you think He wants to grow in you?

———————————— ✠ ————————————

*Dear heavenly Father, continue to do all that needs to be done
for me to be fruitful for You. In Jesus' name. Amen.*

When Dreams Come True

Although Joseph recognized his brothers, they did not
recognize him. Then he remembered his dreams about them.
GENESIS 42:8-9

*P*eople can get used to watching you go through trials so they don't
recognize the change in you when it occurs. And perhaps they don't
want to. To acknowledge your transformation may magnify all they are not.
The same people who couldn't (or wouldn't) dream with you will surely see
your dream come to pass...but not for the reasons we may think. Now is
not the time to say, "I told you so." Instead, give God thanks for all that
He's done. Thank Him for being faithful. Praise Him that He sustained
you through the seasons that shook your faith at times. And as you thank
Him, ask Him to put your realized dream in perspective once again. Resist
the temptation to proudly hold your fulfillment over the heads of others.
Everyone isn't where you are. So thank God you are in your space and leave
it at that.

What is your natural instinct when others have failed to believe with
you? How can you share your fulfilled dream with grace?

---

*Dear heavenly Father, help me remember that life is not about
proving a point. Life is about doing Your will. In Jesus' name.
Amen.*

Our Motives

And now, do not be distressed and do not be angry with
yourselves for selling me here, because it was to save lives
that God sent me ahead of you...God sent me ahead of you
to preserve for you a remnant on earth and to save your lives
by a great deliverance...So then, it was not you
who sent me here, but God.

GENESIS 45:5,7-8

No one can do anything to us that God doesn't allow. Every trial has to get past God's desk before it can be initiated. As we mature in the things of God, one of the first lessons we learn is nothing is as it seems. Few things are for the purpose we thought they were. God planted the dream in Joseph's heart about his brothers bowing before him. Joseph didn't really know what it meant or what would happen. In fact, he may have looked forward to it's unfolding because of his desire to be respected, loved, and accepted by his siblings. But God had a greater purpose. He was going to save a nation!

As we lay our dreams at the feet of Jesus and allow Him to breathe on them, we gain clarity and the motivations of our hearts are rearranged. Our passion needs to align with God's before our dreams can unfold in the greatness God intends. And yes, it is all good. The waiting will be worth it when the dream unfolds, and the tests will transform into testimonies that give glory to God.

What purpose is God working toward in your life?

Dear heavenly Father, empty me of my own agenda so I can be totally sold out to Your purpose. In Jesus' name. Amen.

What Are We
Really Searching For?

What are you really seeking? Love? Fulfillment? Peace? Joy? A sense of well-being? Where are you looking for these things? Have you noticed that the more you seek these things in people the more dissatisfied you become?

Most of us have spent too much time looking in the wrong places for what only God can provide. He has promised that if we don't grow weary of well-doing, we will reap bountifully. He encourages us to know who He is and that He rewards those who diligently seek Him. Did you get that? Those who *seek Him.*

And what is the ultimate prize? God is our reward! When He comes on the scene He brings everything we desire and showers us with it as we get caught up in His embrace. And that's when the full understanding that He is our all, our everything, finally becomes a reality. At last we cease from our struggles and rest totally in the love we've been searching for.

Where Your Heart Is...

And God spoke all these words: "I am the LORD your God,
who brought you out of Egypt, out of the land of slavery.
You shall have no other gods before me."

EXODUS 20:1-3

A preacher once said that he believes one of God's favorite feats was releasing the children of Israel and bringing them through the Red Sea because God brings it up repeatedly in His Word. If He updated His message for the present day, I believe He would say, "I am the LORD your God, who brought you out of the slavery of sin. I caused you to pass from death to life through the blood of my Son, Jesus. You shall have no other gods before Me."

What does God mean by "gods"? He's referring to anything that takes up more of our minds, hearts, and spirit space than He does. That includes men, careers, possessions, and more. He's referring to anything that vies with Him for our heart affections and our soul worship.

Humans tend to worship what we feel we can't live without. "Where [our] treasure is, there [our] heart will be also" (Luke 12:34). What I think I *must have* is a god if it isn't my heavenly Father. There's no way around this. We offend God when we put anything before Him on our priority list.

God provided for His people in the ancient days, and He does the same now. If you made the ultimate sacrifice of whatever was most precious to you for the sake of a person and they decided they loved something more how would you feel? I thought so. God has every right to ask for our single-hearted devotion. He has earned it.

What things or people fight for your heart's attention?

——————————————— �֍ ———————————————

Dear heavenly Father, forgive me for the times my heart strays. I long to be wholeheartedly devoted to You. In Jesus' name. Amen.

An Undivided Heart

Love the LORD your God with all your heart
and with all your soul and with all your strength.
DEUTERONOMY 6:5

[Jesus said,] "Love the Lord your God with all your heart and with
all your soul and with all your strength and with all your mind."
LUKE 10:27

God wants all of us, plain and simple. And not just our hearts—He wants our minds too. He knows our hearts will follow whatever we decide. The mind is the driver; the heart is the influencer. These two can do a dangerous dance together. The heart is deceitful and tries to convince the mind to follow it (Jeremiah 17:9). However, when our minds make decisions, our hearts usually line up with it. Our flesh tugs at our hearts, demanding what it wants to satisfy its cravings. And if we're weak and don't call on God for help...well, it's all over but the repenting.

God wants all of us because a house divided against itself cannot stand. We will fall over at the first "sweet nothing" whispered in our ears...at the first offer that looks good without reading the fine print. "With all our strength" means the full weight of our decision to guard our hearts and not let anything distract us from loving God completely. He is the one true thing in life that will always yield a return for our investment above and beyond what we put in. He is the only basket safe enough to put all our eggs in. He wants all of us to be for all of Him.

Trust me. We get more out of the deal than He does!

Where is your heart today? What distracts and divides your affection toward God? How safe and sure are the other things you're trusting in?

——————————————— ⁜ ———————————————

Dear heavenly Father, forgive me for the times my heart has been divided. Help me love You with all that is within me. In Jesus' name. Amen.

Looking in the Mirror

Love your neighbor as yourself. I am the LORD.
LEVITICUS 19:18

Today I felt fat, and I admit I wasn't gracious toward a woman who was thin. She was an unpleasant reminder of what I need to lose. A famous comedienne wrote a book called *Skinny People Are Evil*. I laughed when I saw the title but so understood the sentiment. Isn't it amazing how our evaluation of ourselves colors our attitudes toward others?

God's command to love others as we love ourselves is not about ego. No, it's about finding a healthy balance between being aware of our faults and celebrating the people God created us to be. As we walk in the confidence that God created us, called us "good," and gave us the capability to bless others because of how He's made us, we are set free to celebrate others. No comparisons are needed because we are all uniquely made and crafted to add something special to the whole. But we are only able to love others as much as we love ourselves. So let's consider ourselves carefully and honestly. We need to dwell on the positive and honor who God created us to be. We can treat ourselves well...and then spread the love.

How do you feel about you? How does this manifest in the way you treat yourself? In how you treat others?

———————————— ✠ ————————————

Dear heavenly Father, help me see myself through Your eyes.
In Jesus' name. Amen.

Supernatural Supply

Then the LORD said to Moses,
"I will rain down bread from heaven for you."

EXODUS 16:4

One of the scariest things about being single is a question that looms in the back of our minds: "How will I be taken care of?" Little girls are conditioned early to dream of white knights, awesome and fabulous, appearing over the horizon on a magnificent steed, sweeping them off their feet, and carrying them away to a land where everything is wonderful, beautiful, and plenteous.

We all have our Cinderella dreams, and yet we're rudely awakened by the reality of our singleness and the years going by with no sign of our princes in sight. And yet we do have a Prince who has promised to be our Jehovah-jireh, our faithful provider. He will supernaturally supply all we need, which is often different than our wants, according to His riches in Christ Jesus (Philippians 4:19). Materially, spiritually, and physically, God will take care of us. He'll provide food for our bodies and food for our souls. His supply never runs out.

We could marry wealthy men today, and they could lose all their money tomorrow. But our God will never fail to pour out the sustenance we need on a daily basis. We may not always see or know the source, but God is faithful.

What are your needs today? In what ways is God meeting your needs?

---- ❖ ----

Dear heavenly Father, when I'm hungry, please be my sustenance. In Jesus' name. Amen.

Our Daily Bread

[The LORD said,] "The people are to go out each day
and gather enough [bread] for that day. In this way
I will test them and see whether they will follow my instructions."
EXODUS 16:4

God followed through on His word and rained bread down from heaven for the Israelites. The Israelites called the bread "manna." Have you gone through "manna seasons"? These are times where provision and blessing are given in measured amounts so we keep going back to the Lord.

Jesus taught us to pray, "Give us today our daily bread" (Matthew 6:9). Perhaps if God gave us enough for the week, He wouldn't hear from us again until the provisions ran out. For example, when I walk my two dogs, I keep them on leashes. However, every now and then I let them free to see if they will wander. One does and one doesn't. I know which one I can trust to remain obedient no matter what distractions come its way. God also tests us. Not because He doesn't know what we'll do, but because He wants us to see the conditions of our hearts. He wants us to know how prone we are to wander if we don't get into the habit of seeking Him for everything. Our obedience and submission are tied to whom we view as our main source.

God must be our primary source for all things—love, finances, validation, whatever we need. All other sources are sure to disappoint eventually. Only God has an endless supply.

How is your daily walk with God? What distracts you and causes you to wander away from daily dependence on Him?

_____ ✠ _____

Dear heavenly Father, forgive my wandering heart. Teach me how to draw close to You consistently. In Jesus' name. Amen.

In Desert Places

They looked toward the desert, and there was
the glory of the LORD appearing in the cloud.
EXODUS 16:10

Sad to say, but most of us don't seek God until we are in hard places. In arid places devoid of signs of life or the things we've been longing for. God waits for us in those deserts.

Our natural tendency is to feel deserted by God, to stop communicating with Him, and to look for sustenance in other areas. He patiently waits until our souls are parched with unfulfillment and longing and we cry out to Him. Then He leads us to a place of refreshing water. This is where His glory shines, and we gain glimpses of His heart we wouldn't get to see elsewhere.

In the desert places of our lives we need to keep moving forward by depending on God to help us. When our spirits are dry and our hearts are empty, we can look to Him. Redemption is on the way! However we must seek Him. Preferably we learn to do this early in our wanderings, but even if it's late we can always turn to Him. When we seek Him, we will find Him. And He will come, bringing all we need.

What do the desert times in your life look like? How can you remember to call on God in these times?

———————————————— ⋈ ————————————————

Dear heavenly Father, I am thirsty. Refresh me with You. In Jesus' name. Amen.

Food for Tomorrow

[The LORD said to Moses,] "Bear in mind that the LORD
has given you the Sabbath; that is why on the sixth day
he gives you bread for two days."...So the people
rested on the seventh day.

EXODUS 16:29-30

I love God. He thinks of everything. He is so concerned about our care that He thinks of every little detail, including our rest, our provision, and even things we don't think of. God has made this provision part of His divine design for us.

God rained down bread from heaven for the children of Israel every day for 40 years when they were wandering in the desert. He told them to only gather enough for the day. But some didn't trust Him to provide every day so they gathered extra and hoarded it. When they went to eat it the next day, it was spoiled and wormy! However, God told them to gather extra manna on the sixth day to honor the Sabbath day of rest. He didn't want them to worry about what they would eat on that day, so He provided enough.

God is faithful! He will provide for us. And that, my friend, gives us rest.

What do you worry about? How can you reassure yourself that God will provide?

------------------------------ ✠ ------------------------------

Dear heavenly Father, help me trust in You for everything concerning me. When I doubt You, remind me of Your promises and how You always keep them. In Jesus' name. Amen.

The Trouble with Trust

Trust in the LORD with all your heart
and lean not on your own understanding.
PROVERBS 3:5

Sometimes it's hard to separate our hearts from our minds, and yet we must. We tend to lean on our intellectual perceptions, which are limited to what we can interpret. But when we truly love the Lord, we trust Him and His intentions toward us. How many times does He have to say to us, "I know the plans I have for you...Plans to prosper you...plans to give you hope and a future" before we get it? (See Jeremiah 29:11.)

The trouble is that even though He knows, we doubt. And so we fret. We haven't gotten to the place where we entirely trust His agenda for our lives. We can't conceive that His perfect will can make us happy and fulfilled. Sad but true, isn't it? We're suspicious of God. We fear He won't give us the desires of our hearts. We don't trust that He will provide everything we need.

Oh, the garden path the enemy can lead our minds down when we falter in trusting God! Our limited capacity can never imagine all that God has planned for us, but we can rest and trust in the fact that He is looking out for us and wants what's best for us. We can remember all His promises and how He's kept every one. He is trustworthy and loves us. And that's all we really need to remember.

What makes your trust in God waver? What do you need to understand to be more consistent in your faith?

———————————— ⊡⊡ ————————————

Dear heavenly Father, I struggle between the visible and the invisible. Help my unbelief. In Jesus' name. Amen.

The Straight Path

In all your ways acknowledge him,
and he will make your paths straight.
PROVERBS 3:6

It doesn't take much to get off the pavement on the road of life. We only have to be left to our own devices or listen to bad advice from friends. How much simpler would life be if we took the time to check in with the only One who knows best! God made us a tremendous promise, and He always keeps His promises. He said if we acknowledge Him, He will instruct us and make sure we are on the right road and headed toward all that He desires for us, which is ultimately what we want. How beautiful is that?

I've discovered that when I ignore Him I get into trouble. On those days that I pick up the pieces of my life and all my toys, cradle them in my willful arms, and decide I'm going to go my own way, it's usually not long before I go splat in the midst of a mess. As the beautiful old hymn "What a Friend We Have in Jesus" states, "O what peace we often forfeit, O what needless pain we bear, all because we do not carry everything to God in prayer." Does this mean God is interested in every little thing in our lives? I believe it does! I think He is totally delighted when we include Him even in the mundane decisions of life, so passionate is He about having a relationship with us. In *all* our ways...not just some, look to Him. That's when life gets a lot easier.

Which portions of your life do you tend to take on yourself? What is the outcome? In what ways will God's participation help?

Dear heavenly Father, forgive me for my independence. In Jesus' name. Amen.

The Keeper of Your Heart

Above all else, guard your heart, for it is the wellspring of life.
PROVERBS 4:23

Our hearts are our most precious commodity. We shouldn't play with them or treat them carelessly. Our heart condition affects every area of our lives. No wonder God admonishes us to be careful!

No one will take better care of your heart than you because it is yours. So be careful where you place it and who you entrust it too. Careless people may play, manipulate, hurt, and exploit your heart, and you'll be left to deal with the damage. If strangers are visiting my home, I don't leave the items that are precious to me out in clear view to be touched or taken. I put them in a safe place. Keep your heart in a safe place too. Take the time to discover its value, and then discern who is worthy of knowing it. Your life depends on it.

How has past heartbreak impacted your life? In hindsight, what could you have done differently to ensure the safety of your heart?

Dear heavenly Father, You are my Rock, my strong Tower, my safe Hiding Place. I give You my heart. Help me keep watch over it. In Jesus' name. Amen.

Pray Before You Leap

Make level paths for your feet and take only ways that are firm.
PROVERBS 4:26

The saying "It is better to have loved and lost than not have loved at all" is a great deception in my opinion. God's Word says, "Hope deferred makes the heart sick" (Proverbs 13:12). Therefore, unnecessary heartbreak should be avoided at all costs. And this is within our power to a great extent.

Sometimes desperation for relationship causes us to move unwisely. The safest route for single people is to get to the place of maturity where taking poor risks with our hearts and lives are no longer options. Part of guarding our hearts is taking the time to do our homework *before* we follow our passions.

Hearts are nothing to play with. Why take chances with something so precious? As the apostle Paul said, "When I was a child, I talked like a child, I thought like a child, I reasoned like a child. When I became a man, I put childish ways behind me" (1 Corinthians 13:11). Taking careful thought and consideration are the prerequisites to making sound decisions.

I encourage you to "look before you leap." Prayerfully seek God before making a commitment or getting involved with someone. Remember, looks can be deceiving. As one of my mentors says, "Patience is the tool that uncovers deceit." Take the time to be sure of what you're getting into. You can't always be absolutely sure, but you can diligently take precautions and make informed choices.

What is the best choice you've ever made when it comes to relationships? What is the worst? What was the outcome? What would you do differently now?

Dear heavenly Father, grant me the gift of discernment so I can make wise choices. In Jesus' name. Amen.

Motives

All a man's ways seem innocent to him,
but motives are weighed by the LORD.
PROVERBS 16:2

Why do you want what you want? Perhaps your reasons are what's keeping you from achieving your dreams. I think of Hannah, who longed for a son for years. Only after she promised to surrender her son to the LORD did her womb open and she conceived. Would Hannah have given her son to the Lord if she'd become pregnant the first time she prayed? Perhaps not. Before her decision to dedicate her son to the LORD, having a baby was all about her. Her need to be like other women in Israel. Her need to prove her worth to her husband. To appease her mother-in-law. To silence the neighbors. To be viewed as valuable as her husband's other wife, Peninnah.

Hannah wanted a son, and God wanted a prophet. God's desires for us will always be greater than our desires for ourselves. We're told in the book of James, "You do not have because you do not ask [God]. You ask and do not receive, because you ask with wrong motives, so that you may spend it on your pleasures" (4:3 NASB). Our dreams must be surrendered to God for His glory and not just our consumption. God wants to create something greater than what we envision or desire. So as we lift our hands to Him in prayer, we need to make sure our motives are pure.

Why do you want what you want? How will it benefit you? Other people? God?

Dear heavenly Father, forgive me for my selfishness. Help me see every blessing in light of Your glory. In Jesus' name. Amen.

The Secret to Success

Commit to the LORD whatever you do,
and your plans will succeed.
PROVERBS 16:3

"What do you think?" one of my girlfriends asked. We were discussing her latest love interest. He was not a Christian, and he'd already proven he lacked integrity. Yet the need of my friend's heart for companionship was blinding her to the truth. As I stated what I felt was obvious—that he was not worthy of the position she wanted him to hold in her life—I realized my words were falling on deaf ears. I stopped and shrugged. "It really doesn't matter what I think," I said. "You need to find out what God thinks about your choice."

If what we're considering isn't signed, sealed, and delivered by God, it will not last. "Unless the LORD builds the house, its builders labor in vain" (Psalm 127:1). We can't keep what God doesn't put together. The needless pain most of us heap on ourselves by going our willful ways for the sake of getting what we want should be enough to convince us that success in life begins with submitting all we desire to God. As He shifts our priorities and rearranges our motives, we are placed in position to receive what we desire and to keep it!

What parts of your desires have you refused to give to God? What are you afraid the outcome will be if you submit your desire to Him?

Dear heavenly Father, forgive me for the times I snatch my desires out of Your hands. Help me commit everything to You for Your guidance. In Jesus' name. Amen.

God's Ultimate Will

The LORD works out everything for his own ends.
PROVERBS 16:4

At the end of the day God is still God. So let's not fool ourselves. God *will* have His way. In His omniscience He knows the best way for each of us to take. Long before we were, our days were already counted. In His foreknowledge He stays ahead of us.

At the end of our mistakes, when we reach for Him, He meets us and gets us back on track and on schedule with His divine plan. "In all things God works for the good of those who love him" (Romans 8:28). He works all things for His good, which is ultimately our good. What we must trust is that God's will is what will give us the most joy. Until we settle this issue, we'll struggle against His will and pursue our own. And our paths usually lead to great frustration and angst. Yet in the midst of our disappointment and lack of faith, if we ask, God will meet us, pick up the pieces, and rearrange them in accordance with His will and to our benefit. We find ourselves surprised by joy! Once again God surpasses our wishes with a much better outcome than we dreamed. We are blessed and He is glorified—which is what we all want!

What area of your life are you struggling to figure out? What does God say about it?

———————————— ✠ ————————————

Dear heavenly Father, forgive me for struggling to have my way. Reign in my life today. In Jesus' name. Amen.

The Path to Life

The fear of the LORD leads to life:
Then one rests content, untouched by trouble.
PROVERBS 19:23

When I was a child I feared my mother. The thought of what she would do if she caught me disobeying her "scared me straight." Her invisible presence in my head dictated my choices in spite of the urgings of my peers. That fear has now been replaced with a healthy respect and appreciation for her wise instructions that kept me safe over the years. Can you relate?

Now you and I are adults, free to make our own choices. We encounter crossroads in many instances. Our way or God's way? Will we accept the fact that the choices we make don't lead to healthy and satisfied and fulfilling lives? Often they lead to death…death of the very things we wish for—relationships, careers, dreams. We choose to compromise ourselves to get what we want. But when we choose to have a healthy fear of the Lord, to respect His Word, and to obey His instruction, we find the paths that lead to abundant life and avoid trouble. Doing life God's way is the path to peace where our souls will find rest instead of the pain and turmoil we set ourselves up for. Holiness and godly living will spare us from more trouble than we know.

When you choose your own path, what is your attitude toward God? What is usually the outcome?

———————————————— ✠ ————————————————

Dear heavenly Father, forgive me for choosing to do things my way. Help me stay on the path of life in You. In Jesus' name. Amen.

Who Is Faithful?

Many a man claims to have unfailing love,
but a faithful man who can find?

PROVERBS 20:6

*L*et's face it. There is none faithful save the Lord. This is where we must hide our hearts. Mere men will fail us. Don't blame them. It's their humanity at work. If we're honest, even we've failed someone... and probably several times. We might say, "Charge it to our heads and not our hearts," but the truth remains that we've let someone down. In thought, word, or deed we fail our loved ones again and again.

And yet we can be faithful when submitted to the Spirit of God. His faithfulness becomes our own. In and of ourselves we are incapable of the commitment it takes to be constant and unwavering in our relationships. Where can we find a faithful man? At the foot of the cross.

How faithful have you been? What interrupts your faithfulness to God?

———————————— ✠ ————————————

Dear heavenly Father, let my faithfulness begin with being faithful to You. In Jesus' name. Amen.

Do the Right Thing

To do what is right and just
is more acceptable to the LORD than sacrifice.

PROVERBS 21:3

Many years ago there was a movie titled *Do the Right Thing*. That is certainly easier said than done. A sign of maturity is that we choose the right path...do the right thing. We finally see that a moment of pleasure is not worth all the work it takes on the back end to get back on track. Life is simpler when we follow God's directions in the first place. How many times have we cut corners in our lives only to find that in the end we pay more than we would have if we'd just done the right thing in the first place? Some call it being "penny smart and pound foolish" when it comes to money, but what about when it comes to life?

When we compromise God's standards, we will inevitably find ourselves back at the foot of the cross broken and spent, empty and despairing. Doing the right thing costs us way less and leads to abundant life. God doesn't want us to have to be sorry for our actions. He takes no delight in our pain and suffering. His preference is that we live in victory. That we be free from regret. He is delighted when we joyfully do the right thing the first time out of devotion and love for Him.

What are some of the times when you chose to take shortcuts on what you knew you should do? What price did you pay for your disobedience? What will you do differently next time?

Dear heavenly Father, help me do the right thing for You the first time. I want to be a good witness of You to the people around me. In Jesus' name. Amen.

Becoming a Woman of Worth

A wife of noble character who can find?
She is worth far more than rubies.
PROVERBS 31:10

I firmly believe that on the day the Lord presents me to my husband, my husband will sing praises to God. Why? Because I am doing my homework. I am allowing God to make me into a woman "worth far more than rubies." I have honed my homemaking skills, cooking skills, and all the other skills required to be a blessing to my mate. Because of this, I know my value. I know I am a priceless find. This doesn't mean I think I'm perfect, but I am working to become more like Christ.

One result of this is that I'm much more discerning about men than I used to be. Not only will I be a gift, but my prospective partner will also be a gift to me. I know good and perfect gifts come from God. Not in the sense of perfection as in flawless, but perfect for me, a good match for me, a complement to me. I expect him to have noble character. To be a man of integrity with a heart after God. To be someone who knows how to love me the way Christ loves the church. And because I am what I am in Christ, I will not settle for less. How about you?

What do people say about your character? How are you allowing God to prepare you for marriage? In what ways will you be a blessing to your future mate?

Dear heavenly Father, prepare me for the one You have chosen for me that I might be a blessing. In Jesus' name. Amen.

Timing Is Everything

There is a time for everything, and a season
for every activity under heaven.
ECCLESIASTES 3:1

Life is a series of seasons, and for each season there is a purpose. Knowing and resting in the purpose of the season we're in helps us enjoy that time in our lives. "What would you do if you found out you only had one day to live?" Would your priorities be quickly reorganized? They would certainly be in my life.

Suddenly what is truly important comes to light. As Scripture notes, there is a time for everything. But often we miss enjoying our present moments because we are regretting the past or worrying about the future. One of the greatest things we can master is being present now. That means not wishing anything else is happening other than what is.

Right now, hopefully, you are exactly where you're supposed to be. (If you're not, you need to get where God wants you.) That will only lead to deep frustration. And if you're in a difficult place, remember: Before you know it this too shall pass, and you will be on to something else. So let's revel in the season and take it for what it is. After all, the present is just that—a gift from God.

How can you better enjoy the season you're in? How can you take advantage of where you are now? What are you grateful for right now?

———————————— ❖ ————————————

Dear heavenly Father, forgive me for the times I peer ahead.
Help me to remain present with You. In Jesus' name. Amen.

Setting Boundaries

There is a time for everything...
a time to embrace and a time to refrain.
ECCLESIASTES 3:1,5

Part of guarding our hearts is setting boundaries that keep us safe. Although God has given us hearts filled with passion coupled with hormones and chemistry, He also requires that we control all these things that affect our flesh. While the world is having a free-for-all and sexuality has become a cheap commodity, those who know God understand how costly intimacy can be. We are called to make different choices. To respect our bodies and how God made us. To understand that sexuality and intimacy is a gift from God to be cherished and nurtured and protected.

This means we need to be honest with ourselves about our weaknesses and set boundaries accordingly. The Shulammite woman in Song of Songs said, "Do not arouse or awaken love until it so desires." In other words, until it's the right time. You may think this is funny, but making a soufflé comes to mind. They are so yummy...but so delicate. I have to be careful to take it out of the oven at just the right time or it will fall flat. It can end up not being what it's supposed to be if tampered with prematurely. And so it is with love, our hearts, and our bodies. Too much too soon can rob us of what we desire. There is so much to look forward to in love *if* we take the time to allow things to come to full maturity. God makes everything beautiful in its right time.

Think back to a time when you may have given too much too soon. What was the outcome? In hindsight, what would you do differently?

———————————— ⚜ ————————————

Dear heavenly Father, help me understand the value of my love. Help me discern the right season for sharing what You have created and given me. In Jesus' name. Amen.

Give It Up

There is a time for everything...a time to search and a time
to give up, a time to keep and a time to throw away.

ECCLESIASTES 3:1,6

The day came when I had to settle it once and for all. Could I live as a single woman for the rest of my life and be content? Could I honestly say that if I never got married that would be all right with me and I would still love God just as much if not more? The answer surprised me! Yes. The day came when I said, "Yes, I will be fine. I will be joyful." Wow! It was a liberating moment. The angst of the big *when* was over.

The question of marriage had become a big burden. It grew heavier every time someone I knew got married. It weighed down my spirit and my countenance. And now, in this quiet moment, I made peace with my singleness. No longer was I going to fight against it like I was the unlucky victim of quicksand. I would float on top instead and chart my path, now fully empowered to enjoy life and welcome any surprises I encountered along the way. Marriage would be the cherry on top of the iced cake I already had—if God brought me a mate. It was time to stop looking and hoping and wishing and, instead, give the timing over to God. I would keep the hope but throw the desperation away. I took a deep sigh of relief that at last I owned my desire. It no longer owned me.

What will it take for you to make peace with your singleness? Why do you think this is crucial to marriage preparation? What do you fear most about letting that desire go?

Dear heavenly Father, help me put my desire for marriage in perspective. Help me long for You the most. In Jesus' name. Amen.

The Secret to Fulfillment

The LORD is my shepherd, I shall not be in want.
PSALM 23:1

Have you read the entire Psalm 23? I encourage you to take a minute and do that right now. The psalmist is praising the Lord and what He does for us. The writer says God leads us by calm waters and refreshes our parched souls. He makes us rest in green pastures, lush and plush with all we need to sustain our hungry hearts. He promises to restore our souls when we feel depleted. And God leads us in paths of righteousness, in right-standing with Him, which always leads to our fulfillment, joy, and peace.

Sometimes I have to walk these things out in my mind until the truths sink into my understanding and calm my longings. This is when it becomes clear that left to my own wandering nature I would soon find myself in want. But when I allow the Guardian of my soul to lead me, I am satisfied. I shall not want because I am complete in Him. I shall not be in want because He provides all that I need. Everything else is extraneous and not profitable to my soul or my life. Can you relate?

So choose to walk with Him! Let Him fill you with what He knows is best. Being fulfilled—it's a beautiful feeling.

What do you hunger for? How can you let God fill you and satisfy you?

———————— ⌖ ————————

Dear heavenly Father, help me not to crave anything except what You desire for me. In Jesus' name. Amen.

The Waiting Game

Wait for the LORD; be strong and take heart and wait for the LORD.

PSALM 27:14

I hate waiting. Have you ever noticed when you're going somewhere that you've never been that it seems to take forever to get there? The return trip home never seems as long. When waiting for a specific life event, such as marriage, it's even harder. I think it's the unknown that stretches before us, overwhelming us with its uncertainty. The lack of knowing all the details makes the journey between the promise and the possession of it more overwhelming than it actually is.

The longer we wait, the weaker we get. Resignation sets in, followed by an apathy that is hard to shake. This can turn to paralysis, where we cease to function or pay attention to the things we should. "What are we waiting for?" That's the question in these times. Are we waiting for a mate to appear? For a dream to come true? For a big break? What we are waiting on can heighten our despair.

But Scripture says to wait for the Lord, not wait for what we want. We have no control over life happenings, but God does! And He always delivers what is best for us.

What are you waiting for? Is it within your power to manifest? Where should your attention be right now?

———————— ✠ ————————

*Dear heavenly Father, I am turning my eyes toward You today
and choosing to wait for You. In Jesus' name. Amen.*

It's All Good

The lions may grow weak and hungry,
but those who seek the LORD lack no good thing.
PSALM 34:10

When we get back to our room tonight, let's pray for our husbands," my friend said to me. My stomach sank. That was not on my to-do list for the evening.

"Why?" I asked.

"Well, the Word says that no good thing will God withhold from those who love Him," she answered.

"Hmmm, so doesn't that mean that if He thought it was good for us to have husbands right now, He would have given us them?"

She looked at me in silence.

Needless to say, we didn't pray for husbands that night. I truly believe that if I make the Lord my first priority, everything else will fall into place. God has good taste and impeccable timing. Though others around me might be struggling with their biological clocks, thinking about their ages, and feeling as if they're running out of time, I will seek the Lord. All those other thoughts make us weak and hungry. But those who truly trust the Lord believe He has given them everything they need for right now. Tomorrow may bring an entirely new set of circumstances with different needs, which He will rise to the occasion to supply. But in the "right here and now," as you practice being present in the moment, believe you lack nothing...because if you did, God would supply it.

Have you taken stock of where you are? What do you think you need right now? Do you think God agrees?

Dear heavenly Father, help me rest in Your present provision, knowing that You know all I need for this moment. In Jesus' name. Amen.

Transformed Desires

Delight yourself in the LORD and he will give you
the desires of your heart.
PSALM 37:4

This has got to be one of most misunderstood scriptures in all of creation. How many of us have walked around thinking that God hasn't lived up to this promise? I believe the greater question is, Have we lived up to our part? "Delight yourself in the LORD," it says. This suggests being totally enthralled with Him. Having a good time with Him. And in the midst of such an intimate interchange, our desires will be transformed into His desires.

Have you noticed it's much easier to get something you want from someone if they want you to have it? Jesus said that when we pray in accordance with the will of the Father, we can ask for what we want and it will be given to us. Perhaps, as James says, "When you ask, you do not receive, because you ask with wrong motives" (James 4:3). But when we want what God wants, the windows of heaven open!

I've rearranged my likes and dislikes over the years according to what the man in my life at that time liked. In retrospect, I wonder how much further along I would be if I had applied the same mindset to my relationship with God. How about you?

In what ways do you feel your present desires line up with God's desires for you? Are there some desires you need to take a closer look at?

Dear heavenly Father, as I submit my heart to You, let Your desires be my desires. In Jesus' name. Amen.

The Price of Obedience

Be still before the LORD and wait patiently for him;
do not fret when men succeed in their ways,
when they carry out their wicked schemes.
PSALM 37:7

"Comparison." That word and concept gets us into so much trouble. It affects our heart condition and sets us on the path to envy, jealousy, bitterness, and strife. And probably every evil work in the world. The enemy of our souls is quick to point out that everyone seems to be doing their own thing and not suffering a bit for it. Those who don't care about living a pure life appear to be doing just fine...and even more than just fine. And those who have purposed to live holy lives seem to be getting nowhere. On and on we can lament. And this is when I have to stop and remind myself why I have chosen the path of obedience no matter what it costs. The reason? I love God. I love Him more than the pleasure or "momentary positives" sin might offer.

At the end of the day all the chickens come home to roost. We might never see the end result of a person's waywardness, but the Bible lets us know that at the end of time what people who choose not to follow Christ will face won't be pretty. Appearances are seldom what they seem to be. Therefore, trust God and be still in Him. He is working your life out for you. And when the blessing comes, you will have no regrets attached to it. Pure or right choices will always reap a great reward. Though the vision and hope may tarry, wait for it, for it will surely be manifest and worth the wait.

Have you felt robbed by not getting something you wanted? What comparisons have you made between what others have and what you have?

———————————— ❖ ————————————

Dear heavenly Father, forgive me for those moments when I resent the path You called me to. Help me remember my walk of obedience is based on my love for You. In Jesus' name. Amen.

The Place of Surrender

Be still, and know that I am God.
PSALM 46:10

I don't know about you, but I come from a generation that has a "make it happen" emphasis. To be still goes against every grain of my being. And I've come to realize that my inability to be still may be connected to questioning God. If I believe God is God over all the things I'm struggling with... If I believe He really loves me and wants the best for me... If I believe I will be totally delighted with His plan for me... If I believe all these things, shouldn't I be able to be still?

When I'm "off to the races" to make things happen, am I doubting one of these key areas of God's sovereignty? Am I pushing all the buttons? Throwing everything against the wall to see what sticks? Exhausting every effort to bring my plans and desires to fruition? And never mind that nothing I'm doing seems to be working. Nothing beats a try but failure, right?

How sad that it takes coming to the end of myself...and often sporting a few unnecessary bruises...to finally open my hands and sit at my Lord's feet, too exhausted to do anything but be still in His presence with a contrite heart. And then He sets my life right again.

I thank the Lord that I'm finally becoming spiritually mature enough to make being still before my Lord my first option of "action" in a situation.

What is your greatest fear about being still? Why do you feel the need to take life into your own hands? In what areas do you need to grow in trusting God?

Dear heavenly Father, grant me the peace I need to be still in Jesus. In Your Son's name I pray. Amen.

The Struggle Within

Create in me a pure heart, O God,
and renew a steadfast spirit within me.

PSALM 51:10

I've often confessed that my heart is a giant garbage can. Try as I might to scrub my mind and cleanse my heart, I fail. I waver between having a good day and plummeting into the abyss of being critical, judgmental, and exhibiting a bad attitude when things don't go my way. And it's even worse if I see others making progress while using less discipline. I find it hard to stick to the path God has called me to, and yet I know that I must not grow weary of well-doing because God has promised that in due season I will reap. I must remain steadfast.

This is where the battle for our minds begins. Satan knows if he can get us to be discouraged, our hearts will be littered with indecision and lack of focus, which will impede or even halt our progress. And this leads to even greater discouragement. The bitter cycle has begun. I believe this is why we need to constantly be renewed in Jesus. The struggle to remain upbeat during difficulties is common to all people on this journey we call life. It's hard to pick ourselves up and get back into the race. We need to remember that in those places and times when we grow weary of running, our loving God will carry us. He remains faithful even when we waver or give in.

In what areas do you feel yourself losing focus and getting off track? What attitudes need to be readjusted for you to have a pure heart?

———————————— �֎ ————————————

Dear heavenly Father, forgive me when I question what You're doing in my life. Plant me in a firm place so I can continue to be steadfast in You. In Jesus' name. Amen.

The Power of Letting Go

Cast your cares on the LORD and he will
sustain you; he will never let the righteous fall.

PSALM 55:22

*A*re you loaded down with cares? Where can you take them? What can you do with them? How long have you carried them and found no solution? Now you know what to do! "Cast your cares on the LORD"! He is able to take the weight. He will sift through the debris and make sense of the things you don't understand or can't fathom. He is able to help you keep what is committed to Him and toss the rest. Let Him have all the things you can do nothing about. He will take care of them. He will take care of you. He can't and won't fail you! And He wants you to succeed. He is your greatest cheerleader! But you must empty your heart and arms to make room for His care. Cast your burdens on Him. Throw them as far as you need to. Let go of your burdens. There is no safer place for your cares than at Jesus' feet.

What do you have a difficult time letting go of? What do you fear will happen if you let go and give it to God?

Dear heavenly Father, I struggle with letting go far too often. Help me find a place of rest by releasing my cares to You. In Jesus' name. Amen.

The Safety of Community

God sets the lonely in families,
he leads forth the prisoners with singing.

PSALM 68:6

They say you can choose your friends, but you can't choose your family. That is only semi true. Through Christ we are joined into a greater family—the family of God. There is no excuse for loneliness now. We are surrounded by a host of those who are running to get the same prize. People who struggle with the same issues we do. People who are nurturing the same faith. This is fellowship at its best. When we share our common circumstances and support one another we grow stronger together.

Community is crucial for singles. Involvement with others is the life-blood of existence. It keeps us from becoming selfish. It's called "getting over yourself." Realizing we aren't alone in our quest for godliness and the things we desire girds us up and gives us strength to keep going. Knowing we're not alone helps us be free to experience life to the fullest. Feeling lonely? Reach out to someone. Find someone to bless! And allow yourself to find freedom where you are.

What type of support system do you have? How accountable to your inner circle are you? How trapped do you feel when you're self-involved? What happens when you focus on others?

Dear heavenly Father, help me find joy in the community of people who believe in You. Give me opportunities to reach out to others in Your name. In Jesus' name. Amen.

The Master Builder

Unless the LORD builds the house, its builders labor
in vain. Unless the LORD watches over the city,
the watchmen stand guard in vain.

PSALM 127:1

*L*et's face it. If we wanted to be married or have a relationship with a man, we could. If we're in the mindset to settle for anything, finding people to spend our lives with is easy. Many singles have chosen to move ahead of God and create their own relationship opportunities. Finding a man is easy, but keeping him is a whole different issue.

When we are the creators of something in this life, its outcome is questionable and not guaranteed. In fact, it will surely fail...eventually. But if God is the author of our relationships, careers, dreams, He is able to keep everything going and make everything succeed. The question then becomes, Do I trust God to prepare a man for me if that's His will? And not, Do I trust that I can find a man?

In trusting God, we must also keep faith when life doesn't seem to be working out as we want it to. We choose to believe He is up to something that will work for our good. He specializes in excavations and redecorating. If we remember this, we allow Him to do what He does best—create a life we will rejoice in living.

What matters have you taken into your own hands? How can you give them back to God?

———————————— ✠ ————————————

Dear heavenly Father, I release all I've been trying to build into Your care. In Jesus' name. Amen.

The Source of Fulfillment

You open your hand and satisfy the desires of every living thing.
PSALM 145:16

What an awesome principle! When God opens His hand and shares what He holds, we will be satisfied. Most of us look for love and fulfillment in the wrong places. We search for satisfaction in the hands of people, who are not equipped to satisfy our deepest longings. We drink from their hands and come up wanting. Could this be why discontentment is so rampant? But God has living water that He gives to all who come to Him thirsty and ask for refreshment. He has a perpetual spring that fills and refreshes according to our needs. He is the only one who knows us and understands our needs and desires. He alone knows how to satisfy us to our very core. At times we can't even express exactly what we need to make life worthwhile. And how much harder it would be to explain to someone else who is as limited by their humanity as we are! But God is aware of every detail and able to fill the empty spaces within us with Himself. He is everything we desire. When we open our hearts, He opens His hands.

What is your deepest desire? Why not go to God today and ask Him to fill your need?

———————————— ⋈ ————————————

Dear heavenly Father, fill the places in me that no one else can fill. In Jesus' name. Amen.

Where Do You Place Your Trust?

Do not put your trust in princes, in mortal men, who cannot save.
PSALM 146:3

So much for fantasies of knights on white horses and princes coming to carry us away. Men are just men. They're locked in the limitations of their humanity like we are. Though it may not be their intention, they will fail us time after time. And God allows them to because He wants us to acknowledge that He alone is God. He will not let anyone else be our "all in all." He will not share His glory with another being.

In guarding our hearts, we must be careful not to make mere men gods or make marriage an idol. This is a setup for major disappointment. Our trust rests in God alone. He is the only Perfect One. The only One true to His word, fulfilling His every promise. He is omniscient, omnipotent, creator of the universe. He is in control at all times, slow to anger, patient and true, ever faithful. He can deliver our souls from hell literally and figuratively. No man can live up to Him.

Have you placed your trust in a mortal? Were your expectations realistic? What did you learn from the experience?

Dear heavenly Father, You are the only one I can truly trust. Thank You for being faithful. In Jesus' name. Amen.

Silencing the Biological Clock

"Sing, O barren woman, you who never bore a child;
burst into song, shout for joy, you who were never in labor;
because more are the children of the desolate woman
than of her who has a husband," says the LORD.

ISAIAH 54:1

A while back I got a letter from a friend of a young lady who was struggling with her biological clock. Her friend was considering artificial insemination. The letter writer was up in arms because she felt this was inappropriate for a single woman to do. So she wrote to ask my opinion. I wrote her back, noting that whenever a woman in Scripture forced the baby issue, it led to chaos. For instance, look at the states of Israel and Palestine, which is a continuation of the conflict between Isaac and Ishmael. Little did Sarah know the havoc she was creating when she urged her husband, Abraham, to sleep with the maidservant Hagar.

The friend of the letter writer wrote me back, telling me how much she loved children and how busy she was mentoring, fostering, and being involved with a children's ministry at her church. I asked, "If you had your own child, would you be as involved in the lives of so many other children who needed you?" She responded, "No." I suggested that perhaps in God's economy she was exactly where she needed to be. God was using her love for children to reach out to many in need instead of just one.

Have you overlooked anyone in your quest for what you want? What other ways can your need for love be met through serving others?

Dear heavenly Father, show me the people You'd like me to be a blessing to. In Jesus' name. Amen.

The True Lover of Your Soul

For your Maker is your husband—the LORD Almighty
is his name—the Holy One of Israel is your Redeemer;
he is called the God of all the earth.

ISAIAH 54:5

No one is really single. Think big picture. This world is not our home. We are in transit and on an exciting journey. But the best part is we collectively make up the bride of Christ. View yourself as a well-kept woman preparing for her wedding day. When the Shulammite woman in Song of Songs was asked why the man she was seeking was better than any other, she had a list of descriptives that made all the other women want to help her find him.

Do you have a description of the Lover of your soul? One day my agent asked me if I had a man in my life. I told her I did. She questioned me about him. I told her that my man was very wealthy. She asked me what he did. I told her he did a bit of everything. She asked where he got his money from. I told her he was into real estate—owned everything. I then went on to describe him in full. He was faithful, never lied, always on time, was never too busy to take my call, supplied all of my needs, was the perfect companion. She wanted to know why she hadn't met him yet. I told her he was off building me a house. She wanted to know when he would be back. I told her any day now. Yes, you guessed it! Jesus is my man. He's the only man I know who can have thousands of women and still manage to make me feel like the only one. Single? Nope. I'm engaged.

What is your status?

———————————— ✠ ————————————

Dear heavenly Father, You are the perfect Matchmaker. I am honored to be part of the bride of Christ. In Jesus' name. Amen.

Father Knows Best

"For my thoughts are not your thoughts,
neither are your ways my ways," declares the LORD.
ISAIAH 55:8

There is so much of this life we have yet to figure out. We base our conclusions about our world on our limited knowledge. Yet in the Spirit, things look very different. God's thoughts are higher than our thoughts because He has a better point of view. He is very purposeful in all He allows.

Often I've wondered why God has allowed me to remain single for so long. But looking back now, I see His wisdom. For every man I thought I would die without, God knew that man would kill something inside me. God's prevention was my protection. At the time I didn't want God's perspective. I wanted what I wanted, not knowing the full scope of what I was dealing with.

And sometimes I've questioned why God does things the way He does. The answer is because He knows what is needed to get the results He wants.

And so I came to the place where I accepted that I may not always agree with what God does, but I know it's best to yield to Him because He knows all and perfects all things concerning me. Simply put, God knows best.

Have you accepted this? In retrospect, what "aha moment" have you had about something God allowed in your life?

Heavenly Father, forgive me for the times I've questioned Your motives. Day by day I learn more about Your wisdom. Thank You for loving me. In Jesus' name. Amen.

Becoming

You know that the testing of your faith develops perseverance.
Perseverance must finish its work so that you may be
mature and complete, not lacking anything.
JAMES 1:3-4

If God never gave you a mate, would you still persevere in the faith? Big question, isn't it? But it's one that needs to be answered. As we walk this journey with Christ, our faith will be tried again and again. And not just on the mate issue. We'll be tested in every area of our lives. But we don't have to be dismayed! We know God is taking us somewhere. We need to allow Him to finish what He has begun in us.

I encourage you to not despise the process of becoming. I remember when my grandmother would process meat in her kitchen. She took a large chunk of meat and fed it through a grinder. It would come out the other end liquefied. It had been broken down to nothing. She would then add spices and preservatives and repack it. In this form it would last longer than in its natural state. God wants us to have a long shelf life. He wants us to withstand what life throws at us with His help. This can only happen as we remain spiritually strong by faith workouts. Being broken down to be built up again by Christ. We can be strong and resilient, mature, well developed, whole, and lacking nothing. When we submit to God's training, the reward is the power to stand...no matter what.

What area is God developing in you right now?

———————————— ✠ ————————————

Dear heavenly Father, though it may not always be comfortable, I yield to Your training, knowing the finished work will be beautiful. In Jesus' name. Amen.

The Path to Maturity

We know that suffering produces perseverance;
perseverance, character; and character, hope. And hope
does not disappoint us, because God has poured out his love
into our hearts by the Holy Spirit, whom he has given us.

ROMANS 5:3-4

"No pain, no gain" is the saying. There is truth to that. Take a look around you. Those who have suffered much have a sweetness and grace that draws people to them. They possess a quiet strength. "A knowing," if you will, that if they made it through the last trial surely they will make it through this small thing. Only the experiences of overcoming in Christ can birth unshakeable, unwavering hope.

Take a look at those who have led an easy, fairly trouble-free life. At the first sign of trouble they fold. They haven't developed backbone. But those who have been through trials have stories to tell and can laugh at trouble. They tell people with confidence born of experience that troubles don't last. They have learned about the love and faithfulness of God the hard way. These are the people God can use mightily. And He does!

What occurrences in your life have made you stronger?

———————————— ✥ ————————————

Dear heavenly Father, thank You for Your faithful wounds. May I become all that You created me to be. In Jesus' name. Amen.

Breaking the Cycle

Awake, awake, O Zion...The uncircumcised
and defiled will not enter you again.
ISAIAH 52:1

There comes a time in life when God is ready to turn the pages in our lives and do new things. For many women who have consistently attracted the wrong men, drama after drama and repeat cycles of painful issues consume their lives. God finally says, "Enough! A new day is here. No more shall these things come nigh you."

If it is true that we are what we attract, God must work in us so we'll attract the man He has for us. The work must begin in our hearts. Our desires must be rearranged until we crave what God wants us to...until we no longer find unhealthy or immature men attractive.

For a long time I attracted commitment-phobic men. This baffled me. After all, couldn't they see that I was to be taken seriously? After much prayer, God revealed to me the depth of my own heart condition. He showed me the fears that made *me* anxious about making commitments. Then I realized I was attracting those who wouldn't upset *my* emotional equilibrium. As God healed my heart, I began to be attracted to a different type of man.

This change was difficult for me to face at first, but it's been very liberating and healthy. Change begins with us...from the inside out...with God's help and love.

What have you been attracting in your life? What do you think God is saying to you?

Dear heavenly Father, I open my heart for You to do the work that is needed so I can experience positive change in my life. Help me be attracted to the people You want me to know. In Jesus' name. Amen.

From Victim to Victor

Shake off your dust; rise up, sit enthroned, O Jerusalem.
Free yourself from the chains on your neck,
O captive Daughter of Zion.
ISAIAH 52:2

The story is told about an old mule that fell down a hole. The hole was so deep the farmer decided his animal was as good as dead. He began throwing in dirt to bury the mule. Every time he threw in a shovel full of dirt, the mule would shake it off and step on the dirt. This continued until the mule was able to get out of the hole!

What lesson can we take from this mule? There's no need to stay bowed over about the disappointments of life and love lost. Contemplate it. Shake it off. Get on top of it. Put it behind you. Use the knowledge to avoid it again. Make decisions that enable you to move on. God does His part by furnishing us with the wisdom and strength we need to survive and grow. It is up to us to use it.

Release yourself from captivity. You don't have time to be bitter. And besides, that only binds you to the offender. Don't let anyone have that much power over your life. You've been called to liberty in Christ. Rise up and embrace it.

What things have you bound? What can you do to free yourself?

———————————————— ✠ ————————————————

Dear heavenly Father, for far too long I have allowed circumstances to victimize me. Today I choose to stand by faith in You and be a victor. In Jesus' name. Amen.

The Path to Completion

The LORD will guide you always; he will satisfy your needs
in a sun-scorched land and will strengthen your frame.
You will be like a well-watered garden, like a spring
whose waters never fail.

ISAIAH 58:11

There is a place of sustenance in Christ that is so sweet! When we find it, we will never thirst again. I don't know the way there except to tell you that it is a path of trial, error, tears, and brokenness. A path of surrender that empties us of ourselves until we say yes to where God is leading us. It's a path that is rich with provision that will surprise us. A place where our needs are satisfied though nothing has necessarily changed externally. We may still be single. We may still be uncertain of where we're going. Everything seems the same, but something has changed. Something on the inside. We are now full. We are now strong. We are now joyous. We are completely satisfied. Our countenances have changed and others have noticed and commented on it. And all we can really do is smile and say, "Finally I've gotten to a place called happy. I'm finally free in Christ. Free to simply be fulfilled in Him."

What areas of dissatisfaction do you need God to transform in your heart? Are you willing to allow Him to be your fulfillment?

Dear heavenly Father, please fill me with You until I want nothing else. In Jesus' name. Amen.

Find Your Rest in Him

If you call the Sabbath a delight and the LORD's holy day
honorable, and if you honor it by not going your own way and not
doing as you please or speaking idle words, then you will find your
joy in the LORD, and I will cause you to ride on the heights of the
land and to feast on the inheritance of your father Jacob.

ISAIAH 58:13-14

*W*eariness opens the door of our souls to be robbed...robbed of all the things God so passionately wants us to have—joy, victory, and a lasting legacy that is rich in all things. All He asks for us to do is come aside and rest a while in Him. To observe the Sabbath. Even God rested on the seventh day. He knew that rest was vital to life. He wants us to delight in being set apart for a day so He can refresh us, rebuild us, and restore us. This is wise!

Rest is crucial to the maintaining of our souls. The rested soul isn't easy prey for deception and bad decisions. No, the refreshed soul is anchored in the soundness of the Lord. The rebuilt soul hears God clearly because the clutter and distraction has been removed. We are full of the Lord through the Word of God and the joy and wisdom He promises.

Are you struggling? Are you depleted physically, emotionally, and spiritually? Come and rest a while in Jesus. Joy comes in being set apart from the clamor.

What is destroying or hindering your ability to rest in God? What do you need to release to embrace His peace?

———————————— ✛ ————————————

Dear heavenly Father, help me find my rest in You. In Jesus'
name. Amen.

"He's not my type," she said.

How many times have we gotten distracted by the wrong type, thinking they were the right one? At the end of the day our flesh must be crucified time and time again until we are attracted to what God finds attractive. For all the times I was attracted to the wrong type I fully realize in hindsight that my chooser was broken because I was still broken inside. I was attracted to what I was—a hopeless commitment phobe. And yet I pined for commitment!

Those who have shattered self-esteem will be attracted to what they think they deserve—someone who reinforces what they unconsciously think of themselves. As we allow God to mend our broken hearts, restore our broken spirits, and let us see ourselves as He sees us, we make healthier choices. In the meantime, our bad choices can take us on a roller-coaster ride to no good end. But there stands God, ready to grab our hands and realign our minds and spirits to Him. He will set us on the sure path to real love and fulfillment.

The Lust of the Eyes

Samson went down to Timnah and saw there a
young Philistine woman. When he returned, he said to
is father and mother, "I have seen a Philistine woman
in Timnah; now get her for me as my wife."

JUDGES 14:1

Our eyes can get us into trouble. Outward appearances aren't always what they seem. A common adage says that men are visual creatures, but the truth is we all are—men and women. Often our desires are driven by what we see. We decide that people are or are not our "type" based on how they look, dress, and so forth. But our eyes can't always be trusted.

Because it's just as easy to fall in love with a nonbeliever as it is to fall in love with a believer, we have a decision to make. The Word of God tells us not to be unequally yoked with unbelievers. But due to what seems to be a shortage of available choices, some people may be tempted to wander beyond the borders of the church or believer-centered organizations to find partners. The question we must ask is, Who do I love most? God or the person we're considering who doesn't share our faith?

What are some of the problems with being with nonbelievers? If they don't share our faith, they won't support our standards, although they may be very accommodating during courtship. It's not fair for us to go into marriage with the intent to "convert" our new mates. They may be planning to change us in this regard too! This is a setup for long-term frustration and pain. So decide ahead of time—choose this day whom you will serve.

How important is it to you that your potential life partner share your faith? What problems are there if he doesn't? Is your potential mate's dedication to God as strong as yours?

Dear heavenly Father, though it is difficult to wait, help me to not compromise my standards. I want to hold out for Your best for me. In Jesus' name. Amen.

The Value of Sound Counsel

His father and mother replied, "Isn't there an acceptable woman among your relatives or among all our people? Must you go to the uncircumcised Philistines to get a wife?" But Samson said to his father, "Get her for me. She's the right one for me." (His parents did not know that this was from the Lord.)

JUDGES 14:3-4

Today's verses are controversial in Christian scholarship. Was Samson supposed to marry a Philistine to carry out God's purpose of confronting the Philistines? Or would God work with Samson's "bad" choice and turn it into an opportunity to confront the Philistines? Regardless of the interpretation, Samson's parents brought up a legitimate concern regarding Samson's choice to go outside his faith for a wife. But Samson insisted.

Sometimes it's hard to listen to others when we want what we want—but we should listen anyway. God uses people to sound alarms when we aren't seeing clearly. When our hearts and flesh are shouting, it's hard to hear the voice of reason above the din. So we need to deliberately quiet ourselves long enough to listen to those whom God has appointed as guardians over us. Parents, saved or unsaved, have our best interest at heart. Close friends whose vision is not clouded by love or infatuation may see things more clearly and can be valuable in the process of weeding out distractions and deceptions from our lives.

I encourage you to listen and heed wise counsel. This may save you many years of heartbreak. In moments like these, pride can become an enemy that refuses to be corrected. Don't listen to its deceptions! Consider the advice given by those who love you, put it before God, and open your heart to hear and receive His direction.

What is your usual response to counsel you don't want to hear?

———————— ❊ ————————

Dear heavenly Father, open my ears to hear what I should hear and silence the parts of me that are tempted to choose unwisely. In Jesus' name. Amen.

The Path to Brokenness

Samson went down to Timnah together with his father and mother.
As they approached the vineyards of Timnah, suddenly
a young lion came roaring toward him.

JUDGES 14:5

Anytime you see the word "down" in Scripture, be aware that something is up. "Down" is not the direction God wants His people to be going. Though we may feel our decisions are personal choices that don't affect anyone else, nothing could be further from the truth. Those who love us usually get dragged down the slippery slope of our disobedience and watch what's happening or even get caught in the disobedience. Sometimes they go along for the ride soundlessly, praying that we will change our direction. Sometimes they sit on the sidelines fearing the consequences that are sure to befall us. In the midst of our dash toward what we want, warnings come that shouldn't be ignored.

Satan is as a roaring lion seeking whom he may devour. Those who are disobedient to God's Word are easy prey. In most instances, God's grace covers us and keeps us safe in spite of ourselves. But don't be mistaken. The silence of God is not necessarily His blessing. It is simply another chance for us to change our minds and get back on His path.

Are you able to discern the warnings God brings to you? Do you let His warnings steer you back on the right path? What happens when you persist in going your way?

———————————— ✣ ————————————

Dear heavenly Father, help me heed Your voice and recognize Your warnings. In Jesus' name. Amen.

The Secrets We Keep

The Spirit of the LORD came upon him in power so that he tore the
lion apart with his bare hands as he might have torn a young goat.
But he told neither his father nor his mother what he had done.

JUDGES 14:6

God's grace is not an escape from what we know to be true and right. His grace gives us an opportunity to choose the right path and please Him. We're not "getting away" with anything when we disobey God. Be clear on that. One of the best ways to check our hearts is to be honest with ourselves about what we are doing and why. Secrets are always a good sign that something isn't quite right. God calls us to openness and transparency.

The unwillingness to walk in accountability speaks volumes. Satan loves isolation because that's when He can do his "best" work. (In Samson's case, he probably kept the killing of the lion a secret because touching the carcass of a dead animal would make him ceremonially "unclean," which would mandate purification and a delay in his marriage.)

In many instances God doesn't allow our sin to do the damage it could. That's because of His love and mercy and grace. But we need to be careful not to mistake the grace of God as a stamp of His blessing on our choices.

Remember in the garden when God questioned Adam after he ate the fruit? He was giving him an opportunity to confess his sin. God leaves room for us to do the same. Unconfessed sin and keeping secrets is a major setup for a fall.

What have you kept hidden out of shame or because of a choice to not walk in purity?

Dear heavenly Father, right now I confess my sins of disobedience to You. [Be specific.] Please forgive me and guide me back to Your path. In Jesus' name. Amen.

Dealing with Dead Issues

Some time later, when he went back to marry her,
he turned aside to look at the lion's carcass. In it was
a swarm of bees and some honey, which he scooped out
with his hands and ate as he went along.

JUDGES 14:8-9

*W*e will most certainly eat the fruit of what we do. When we are on the downward slope from the will of God, we tend to romanticize past events and ignore the reasons why what we did was wrong in the first place.

The honey Samson gathered was inside the carcass. As noted before, touching something dead made Samson "unclean," violating God's law. Yet not only did he touch the honey, he ate it! How many times have we revisited things that are dead issues in our lives, only to pick them up, ingest them, and allow them back into our systems? There they pollute our hearts, minds, and spirits once again.

Isn't it ironic that the same creature that can sting us and cause great pain can also produce something as sweet as honey? And, by the same token, isn't it ironic that sin can provide such a positive feeling...but it's sting brings such serious consequences to our souls and our walk with God?

What are you still clinging to in your life that you need to let go of?

Dear heavenly Father, please help me let go of those habits and actions that aren't conducive to my growth in You. In Jesus' name. Amen.

Breaking the Cycle

When he rejoined his parents, he gave them some,
and they too ate it. But he did not tell them that he had
taken the honey from the lion's carcass.

JUDGES 14:9

The problem with unresolved issues is we tend to make them other people's issues as well. We pollute those we love with the things we refuse to put to rest. Sometimes they have no idea what the source of our anger, criticisms, and insecurities are. They are only privy to the fallout and the effects of our moods and responses to them.

Because we are created as beings who are dependant on one another, our lives intersect and touch in ways that can't be calculated. Nothing that occurs ever affects just one person. Many are touched and sometimes altered by what we suffer. Hurt people hurt other people, and the cycle of pain continues until someone takes the initiative to break the chain of events. This is why it is imperative that we allow the hand of God to heal us and restore us. No one else can be responsible for our healing. It begins with us acknowledging our pain and taking it to the foot of the cross and giving it to Jesus. Then He brings healing and new beginnings.

What has kept you locked in a cycle of pain and unforgiveness? What will it take for you to initiate your healing?

Dear heavenly Father, heal my heart and restore my soul. In Jesus' name. Amen.

The Truth About Love

Then Samson's wife threw herself on him, sobbing, "You hate me! You don't really love me. You've given my people a riddle, but you haven't told me the answer." "I haven't even explained it to my father or mother," he replied, "so why should I explain it to you?"

JUDGES 14:16

There is no place for game playing and manipulation in love. Love never seeks to control the beloved. To surmise that someone doesn't love you simply because he won't bend to your will is to lack a true understanding of love.

Perhaps this same train of thought is what gives some people the wrong view of God? Many believe that if God truly loves them He will give them whatever they want. Nothing could be further from the truth. God's Word tells us that no good and perfect thing will He withhold from those who walk uprightly before Him. His love for us will only allow Him to give what is good for us. But love withholds when necessary for the greater good. Love also frees the Lover to allow the beloved (us!) to respond to Him willingly. To do anything else would be to take advantage of us. Love is not self-seeking. It hopes all things, believes all things, rejoices in the truth, and keeps no secrets. Love is transparent.

What causes you to question if someone loves you? What is your insecurity based on?

Dear heavenly Father, help me to rest secure in Your love, believing that You know and want what is best for me. In Jesus' name. Amen.

The Price of Anger

Burning with anger, he went up to his father's house.
And Samson's wife was given to the friend
who had attended him at his wedding.
JUDGES 14:19-20

*I*n so many instances we don't see the doors we leave wide open for rejection and disappointment. In some instances, we even invite them in by our poor responses to situations! The Word of God tells us to be angry and sin not. So getting angry isn't a sin. And God understands that we get angry. Even He gets angry. But what we *do* with our anger is what dictates our futures. One wrong reaction can cost us much we hold dear.

A brother or sister who has been offended may be harder to penetrate than a fortified city. Though Samson should have been upset by his wife's betrayal, how he handled the situation set him up to lose more than he already had. In many instances, words spoken too quickly and too harshly can never be taken back. Regrets in the wake of misunderstanding can leave irreparable voids in our hearts and lives. So when we're angry, we need to harness our emotions and remain masters over them so they can't destroy what's important to us.

How do you respond when someone offends you? What is the usual outcome from your reaction? Can you do something to get better results?

Dear heavenly Father, help me bring my offenses to You so You can help me make things right. And when someone offends me, help me be forgiving. In Jesus' name. Amen.

The Deception of Revenge

Samson said to them, "This time I have a right
to get even with the Philistines; I will really harm them."

JUDGES 15:3

The work of righting wrongs begins with us. We must examine ourselves to see what part, if any, we played in the misunderstanding. If we find ourselves justifying our behavior, that's a signal that we may not have acknowledged our own weaknesses and sins. This usually leads to wider rifts in our relationships with others and with God. Until we're willing to own our faults and admit how we contributed to the situation either actively or passively, we will fail to grow or make significant progress in our lives.

Sometimes it's not what we say, it's what we don't say. Sometimes it's not what we do, it's what we failed to do that creates problems in our interactions with others. Seeking revenge only deepens our pain and sets us up for more serious repercussions. The refusal to look inward first and respond with maturity comes from a spirit of entitlement and pride. God resists the proud but gives grace to the humble! As we humble ourselves at the foot of the cross and become willing to do the work it takes for true healing, God will always meet us and help us start anew.

In what ways have you sabotaged your relationships in the past? How has misunderstanding widened the rift between you and others? What do you need to do in these instances?

———————————— ❖ ————————————

Heavenly Father, as I humble myself before You, please heal my heart and stop the pain. In Jesus' name. Amen.

The Purpose of Refreshing

Then God opened up the hollow place in Lehi,
and water came out of it. When Samson drank,
his strength returned and he revived.

JUDGES 15:19

In spite of our bad behavior God visits us and revives us. His supply of grace is truly refreshing! Yet in these moments we should not be overconfident. His visitation is not always based on our own merits. Many times it is in spite of us that He comes to wash, fill, and revive us. Why? Because God has His eyes on the big picture of where He is taking us and what He wants to accomplish through us. So He sustains us for His purposes. Lest we use His grace as validation for even more bad behavior, we should beware of not following His standards. God will not be mocked. What we sow we shall also reap—we just never know when.

I encourage you to use the occasion of experiencing God's grace to allow Him to do a greater work in you. As He strengthens you, let Him also change you. Let Him accomplish in you what He has wanted to all along—a complete work of transformation that brings Him glory and blesses you and others.

In those times when God blesses you in spite of yourself, what has been your response?

———————————— ✠ ————————————

*Dear heavenly Father, help me recognize the purpose of Your
grace and respond accordingly. In Jesus' name. Amen.*

The Cycle of Temptation

One day Samson went to Gaza, where he saw a prostitute.
He went in to spend the night with her. The people of Gaza
were told, "Samson is here!" So they surrounded the place
and lay in wait for him all night at the city gate. They made
no move during the night, saying, "At dawn we'll kill him."

JUDGES 16:1

The enemy of our souls is always lying in wait for the opportunity to strike. He waits for us to relax, to settle into a place where we are deceived by the quiet and before the full impact of our choices comes to bear. Samson, like so many of us, seems to have a type of woman he liked. He was swayed off the right path by Philistine women again and again. They were known for their beauty and sensuality.

We too often find ourselves surrounded by those who would tempt us beyond the boundaries God has set to keep our hearts safe. When we wander beyond His instructions, we venture into enemy territory and may find ourselves at the mercy of schemes aimed to destroy us. Satan knows what we like, and he is happy to encourage our wayward desires. He may not necessarily always strike in the dark, but if we wallow in the darkness long enough, even our light will become clouded by it. This is a dangerous state to be in. To love the light of Christ and be protected by it, we must remain in the light, which is beyond the reach of Satan. Only then can we escape harm.

What weaknesses have led you into repeat cycles that endangered your spiritual health? Do you need to take steps to avoid being tempted to revisit them?

Dear heavenly Father, as I submit to You, give me the strength I need to resist the temptations that come my way. In Jesus' name. Amen.

The Path to Bondage

Some time later, he fell in love with a woman
in the Valley of Sorek whose name was Delilah.

JUDGES 16:4

With each step we take in the same direction and away from the will of God, the easier it becomes to embrace the things that are not His will for us. We soon become used to the bondage or chains, and sin becomes our "normal." When others point out where we are deceived, we often turn a deaf ear to their words and intent. We are on a path to great pain and hardship!

In today's verse, the word "Sorek" means "choice vines." Samson had allowed his passions to go unbridled. He chose to be intimate with those he'd been warned against, despising the call of God on his life. So driven was he by his passions and feelings of entitlement that he failed to be grateful when God delivered him from dangerous situations.

Repeat cycles of disobedience are a sure killer of discernment. No discernment; no wisdom. When we turn away from wisdom, we lose the path to a life rich in blessings and communion with God and eventually find ourselves in bondage to sin. In the face of certain temptation, we need to ask, "Who do I love most—what I desire or God?" Only when we make God our greatest love will we find the path back to His light that will lead us in true love and victorious living.

In what areas of your life have you become numb to God's leading and instruction? What battles for your affection and threatens to distract your heart from God?

———————————— ✠ ————————————

Dear heavenly Father, be the protector of my heart and keep me from temptation. In Jesus' name. Amen.

Where Our Strength Lies

So Delilah said to Samson, "Tell me the secret of your great
strength and how you can be tied up and subdued."…
So he told her everything. "No razor has ever been used
on my head," he said, "because I have been a Nazirite set apart
to God since birth. If my head were shaved, my strength would
leave me, and I would become as weak as any other man."

JUDGES 16:6,17

When we don't know the secret to our strength we are vulnerable to fall for anything. To believe that our strength comes from anywhere other than God is gross deception. It is not by our own power or ingenuity that anything is accomplished. We accomplish things solely by the Spirit of the Lord! Our egos can blind us to danger. Samson failed to note that he'd been tricked by a woman to divulge precious secrets before. He learned nothing from his past mistakes because he'd never owned them. He believed it was by his own strength…er pardon me, his hair…that he had overcome his enemies.

Beware! What you put your trust in will fail you if it's not in Christ. And past mistakes will catch up with you, bringing certain reckoning. Perhaps this is why the psalmist was quick to conclude that "God is the strength of my heart and my portion forever" (Psalm 73:26). Amen to that!

Where do you place your confidence? How have those things or people you've trusted in before disappointed you? How can those situations be redeemed?

Dear heavenly Father, I know full well that You are the source of my strength and my life. Be my constant portion. In Jesus' name. Amen.

Heart Issues

When Delilah saw that he had told her everything, she sent word
to the rulers of the Philistines...Having put him to sleep on her lap,
she called a man to shave off the seven braids of his hair, and so
began to subdue him. And his strength left him.

JUDGES 16:18-19

I heard a preacher say once that you should not lay your head down in
the lap of Delilah and expect to get up unscathed. When we relax we
are most vulnerable. The Bible warns us to remain vigilant, stay on guard,
and never lower our defenses because Satan is as a roaming lion seeking
whom he may devour. He needs an opening from us before he can attack
and devour us. Relaxing in the areas where we know we're weak puts us in
position for the enemy to rush us.

Sin lulls us to sleep and makes us spiritually numb. After a while we no
longer sense danger. As Samson slept, Delilah was awake and busy going
about the task of treachery. The people we choose to be intimate with become
a covering to help protect us or a source of exposure to the elements that
can sap us of our strength and harm us. Remember: The person who keeps
your secrets holds your strength. This is why God tells us to guard our hearts
with diligence.

Where do you hide your heart? In what ways is your heart vulnerable to
attack? What do you need to do to secure your heart?

---

*Dear heavenly Father, far too often I give the wrong people
access to my heart. Today I turn to You and ask You to keep
me safe. In Jesus' name. Amen.*

When Grace Runs Out

Then she called, "Samson, the Philistines are upon you!"
He awoke from his sleep and thought, "I'll go out as before and
shake myself free." But he did not know that the LORD had left him.
JUDGES 16:20

The scariest scripture in the Bible in my opinion is this one. When the Lord leaves us, we're in trouble. The grace of our salvation can be intact, but God's protection from the consequences of our choices is not guaranteed. It is conditional on the state of our hearts, which God knows. The unrepentant heart is an unprotected heart. In God's divine knowledge, He knows our ways and our deepest motivations. Based on this, He determines what He will allow in our lives. His constant pursuit of us should guide us back to Him. But if we choose to continue running away from Him, to follow after the things He knows will harm us, He will eventually release us, turning us over to our choices. Then the objects of our desires become our gods, ruling over us. As Scripture says, "Where your treasure is, there your heart will be also" (Matthew 6:21). God will not share His glory with another. If we don't want God, He will not insist on being active in our lives. He will leave us to our own devices and at the mercy of the choices we've embraced. He won't force us to follow Him. The choice is ours.

Do you take for granted God's faithfulness? What would you do differently if you knew He would step back from protecting you? What will it take to get you to obey Him willingly?

Dear heavenly Father, I choose You to be my treasure. Thank You for Your faithfulness and for covering me with Your grace. In Jesus' name. Amen.

True Freedom

Then the Philistines seized him, gouged out his eyes
and took him down to Gaza. Binding him with bronze shackles,
they set him to grinding in the prison.

JUDGES 16:21

When we choose other people and priorities over God, we will end up where we really don't want to be. Generally speaking, the outcome is the same. Our willful choices cause us to be blinded to sin and its consequences, which leads us to the ultimate bondage. When we can't see where we are, we can end up anywhere.

It's all right for us to have desires, but when our desires have us—that's when we are in big trouble. The labor and cost associated with our choices outside of God's will are never worth the work and energy. We're left feeling empty and drained. We feel overworked, underappreciated, and even less valued.

Yet God has called us to experience divine liberty in Jesus. "If the Son sets you free, you will be free indeed" (John 8:36). So why do we struggle with God? Why do we see His commands as harsh restrictions? He is not a tyrannical taskmaster. The enemy of our souls—the devil—is the one who lures us away with promises of fulfillment that lead to imprisonment. Unfortunately, we don't notice we're bound until it's too late! Only in yielding to God can we experience more freedom than we ever dreamed possible. Oh, friend, choose God and find out that He is truly good!

What has imprisoned your emotions? What will it take for you to break free?

Dear heavenly Father, I choose to yield to Your Word for my life. Let me find my liberty in You. In Jesus' name. Amen.

The Gift of Restoration

But the hair on his head began to grow again
after it had been shaved.
JUDGES 16:22

This is one of the things I love most about God. No matter what we've done or experienced, He seeks to reconcile us to Him. There is *always* a chance for restoration. As we call out to the Lord, He is faithful to renew our strength and author new beginnings in our lives.

I know that many people look back on their pasts with shame and wonder how a holy God could ever salvage their lives that were lived so far away from His design. And yet God is tender toward the brokenhearted and those in search of new life. He comes gently and soundlessly, allowing us the room we need to recognize our need for Him. He waits for us to surrender to His beckoning call. This God, who was grieved by our disobedience, is slow to anger and quick to forgive and restore.

As Samson sat in jail pondering his fate, he had a lot of time to take stock of his life and his bad decisions. In that dark time of captivity, God's light became evident to him. His "strength" finally became more about his heart. As Samson's understanding of who God was and who he was in God grew, so did his hair. His strength returned. Mercifully, God is a God of as many chances as we need.

What has stolen your strength? What steps do you need to take to experience God's restoration in your life?

———————————— ✠ ————————————

Dear heavenly Father, I come to You, bringing all the parts of me—broken and whole. Please restore me. In Jesus' name. Amen.

A Life of No Regrets

Then Samson prayed to the LORD, "O Sovereign LORD, remember me. O God, please strengthen me just once more, and let me with one blow get revenge on the Philistines for my two eyes." Then Samson reached toward the two central pillars on which the temple stood. Bracing himself against them, his right hand on the one and his left hand on the other, Samson said, "Let me die with the Philistines!"

JUDGES 16:28-30

Samson's story ends with him killing more Philistines in his death than when he was alive. I don't believe that was God's original ending for him, nevertheless it was the one Samson chose.

Think of all he could have accomplished if he'd had a longer life. We all have free will, and God will not circumvent our choices. There is a powerful lesson to be learned from Samson's life. We can all be more effective if we don't allow ourselves to be distracted by our flesh. We have been given authority over every living thing—and that includes us. Let us use our authority to welcome and heed God's perfect discipline that leads to life, purposeful living, and victory. We get to choose our path—one that leads to a life well lived or one that causes us to look back with regrets.

Jesus came so that we could live life and live it more abundantly than we did before choosing Him. Let's make the best of it.

What regrets do you have about your past? What have you learned to avoid so you keep moving forward in God?

Dear heavenly Father, I give You my past. I also give You my future. Help me make choices that honor You and bless others. In Jesus' name. Amen.

Single, divorced, or widowed—each state of being presents a unique set of challenges. For those who have never been married, the weight of the world is a lot to carry alone. But necessity requires figuring out how to function. Overcoming alone is an art mastered over time.

For the divorced or widowed, making the adjustment to being single again can be harrowing, to say the least. How do we navigate alone through the waters of life when we've been used to having partners help? Those who are single again get to discover what those who have never been married know—God is faithful. He's a constant Partner and Provider who cares for us in miraculous ways.

Ruth, the central person in the book of Ruth, found herself single again, along with her mother-in-law and sister-in-law. Each woman handled her singleness quite differently, proving that it's not so much our state of being but how we respond to what is happening in our world that makes a huge difference in our lives.

The Place of Famine

In the days when the judges ruled, there was a famine in the land.
RUTH 1:1

*W*hen my flesh screams louder than my spirit, I find lack is magnified in my life. The oldest trick in Satan's book is to make us think that God is holding out on us. That God is deliberately withholding our needs and wants from us. Satan tries to get us so focused on something we don't have that we overlook all the things we do have. It's like staring into a mirror. If we look long enough, we'll find something wrong with our faces.

Our flesh will always fail us. Small wonder God said, "Woe to those who trust in the arm of flesh." Provision will run out; strength will be depleted. The flesh is no match for an omnipotent God whose vast supply of all that we need never fails. When the flesh points to the things we lack, we get restless. We forget about God and concoct our own solutions and make impulsive choices based on fear. In today's verse, it's pointed out that this was the time when the judges were ruling in Israel. Pagan worship by the Israelites was rampant. Whenever decisions are based on fear or anger and God is left out of the equation, wrong choices will be made.

For this reason alone we should be still and know that our God is always present and available when the rumble of urgency sounds within us. In Him there is never lack. Without Him our souls are sure to experience famine.

What are you hungry for? In what ways can you get your sustenance from God?

Dear heavenly Father, I am hungry. Fill me with You. In Jesus' name. Amen.

Enemy Territory

A man from Bethlehem in Judah, together with his wife
and two sons, went to live for a while in the country of Moab.
The man's name was Elimelech, his wife's name Naomi,
and the names of his two sons were Mahlon and Kilion.
They were Ephrathites from Bethlehem, Judah.

RUTH 1:1-2

Anytime we feel empty it affects our ability to remain in an attitude of praise. And it's not just single people that feel they suffer from lack. This disease or "dis-ease" also affects married people, and some choose to wander into forbidden territory.

Moab was enemy territory back in Naomi's day. It was known for idolatry, sensuality, and everything God hates. The Moabites were born out of the incestuous exchange between Lot and one of his daughters. They had no regard or respect for God. At one time the king of Moab even bribed a prophet to curse the nation of Israel. And when that didn't work, the women of Moab led the sons of Israel astray through seduction.

Sounds kind of like the world we live in, doesn't it? The deception of "what they thought they should have in the moment" drove Elimelech and his family to leave Judah, cut off their praise of God, and venture to a place they should never have entered. This is called "settling." Yes, we can choose to live anywhere and any way we please. The question is, What will this eventually cost us?

What do you feel is missing from your life right now? What thoughts have you entertained about changing your situation? Are these temporary fixes or do you feel these ideas are God inspired? How is your praise affected when you feel God hasn't answered your prayers?

Dear heavenly Father, in the midst of my need, lead me to the place where I can be nurtured by Your Spirit and kept by Your grace. In Jesus' name. Amen.

The Aftermath of Our Actions

Now Elimelech, Naomi's husband, died, and she was left
with her two sons. They married Moabite women, one named
Orpah and the other Ruth. After they had lived there about
ten years, both Mahlon and Kilion also died, and Naomi
was left without her two sons and her husband.

RUTH 1:3-5

*H*ow interesting. Elimelech (which means "God is my King") moved his family out of Bethlehem because he feared they would die from the famine. The irony that he didn't escape death in this new place of "plenty" can't be overlooked. Whatever we look to as the answer for our lives outside of God will *always* fail us.

We need to conclude that we are not married to anything in this life. Rachel told her husband Jacob, "Give me children or I will die." She died in childbirth. Could it be that God knew the very thing she thought she would die without would be what would kill her? Anything held too dear that is not of God will be our undoing. Elimelech took his wife and two sons to Moab to avoid the famine...to feed their bellies. Elimelech died there. Then the sons married Moabite women. They were "unequally yoked," married to women who didn't worship the one true God. The sons died.

Naomi, along with her daughters-in-law, was left with the fruit of their bad choices. Our choices never affect just us—they affect those around us as well. Sometimes having our way costs more than we can imagine.

What parts of your life have you taken back to live in your own strength? How will your choices stand the test of time?

Dear heavenly Father, please forgive me for the times I've taken my life into my own hands when moved by impatience. Help me trust You and wait on You, in spite of what I don't see. In Jesus' name. Amen.

The Faithfulness of God

When [Naomi] heard in Moab that the LORD had come to
the aid of his people by providing food for them, Naomi and
her daughters-in-law prepared to return home from there.
RUTH 1:6

God is faithful—no matter what we think at times. No matter what we see or don't see, God has His own way of providing for His people. Whether it relates to the economy of finance or romance, God remains faithful. There will always be skeptics and alarmists who will magnify the seeming lack in our lives. If we accept and digest what they feed us, we'll become hungrier.

Someone told me once that a specific lip balm had ingredients in it that actually make lips dry, so customers used more of it. This is what outside influences can do. They spur us on and lead us to places of greater need. Those who stay where God puts them will be fed and satisfied.

Eventually we see the sharp contrast between Naomi's family that struck out to Moab because they couldn't "see" their needs being met in Bethlehem (which means "house of bread"), the place of provision from God. This does not stop God from doing what He does best—meeting people at their place of need. This is why He cries out to us, "Why spend money on what is not bread, and your labor on what does not satisfy? Listen, listen to me, and eat what is good, and your soul will delight in the richest of fare" (Isaiah 55:2). Eventually, if we are smart, we'll find our way back to where our souls are truly fed—back to God.

What substitutes have you settled for? What will it take for you to get back to basics and allow God to feed and fill you?

Dear heavenly Father, forgive me for the times I've settled for crumbs when I could have eaten Your bread. In Jesus' name. Amen.

The Path to Blessing

With her two daughters-in-law she left the place where
she had been living and set out on the road that
would take them back to the land of Judah.

RUTH 1:7

Sometimes we just need to start over. We need to turn to God and ask Him to take us back to the place in our hearts where we first accepted Jesus. After setting out on our own, doing our own thing, and suffering the bitter consequences, we need to return to our first love.

Sometimes geography—physical and mental—has everything to do with our blessing. Where we are may be the hindrance to receiving what God wants to give us. Though change may be difficult and traumatic, we have to decide how badly we want what we want and how willing we are to do what we need to do to get it. We get in our own way more than we know. Our insistence on remaining where we are can rob us of where we want to go.

Let's return to our first love for Jesus, when we were on fire for Him. Let's give Him praise and worship and have grateful hearts in spite of our circumstances. As we seek God on exactly where we should be, we can remain open to His direction and then follow where He points. His paths always lead to blessings!

Where are you right now? Where would you like to be? What will it take for you to get there?

---

*Dear heavenly Father, grant me direction. Show me the way I
should go. In Jesus' name. Amen.*

The Fruit of Our Choices

"Don't call me Naomi," she told them. "Call me Mara, because the Almighty has made my life very bitter. I went away full, but the LORD has brought me back empty. Why call me Naomi? The LORD has afflicted me; the Almighty has brought misfortune upon me."

RUTH 1:20-21

How quick we are to blame God for the circumstances that arise in our lives based on choices we made. Is that really fair? When life assaults us, we can choose to get better, not bitter. Better from the knowledge we gain through the experience—no matter how bad it is.

Yes, sometimes we take a wrong turn, but what can we learn from it? We need to own our bad decisions and mistakes and allow the lessons learned to strengthen us and keep us from taking that path again. Let's face it, God made us free agents. He doesn't stand in our way and bar us from our choices, although I'm sure sometimes He would love to. After all, that's why He gave us His Word in the first place! So we wouldn't make choices that He knows would hurt us. When we choose to go our own way, He stands ready to help us turn around, ready to heal us, and ready to restore our brokenness. But that can only occur if we are willing to own the choices we made, repent, and allow Him to redirect us.

What have you blamed God for in the past that you should own? What have you learned from your choices? What would you do differently next time?

Dear heavenly Father, today I choose to own my bad decisions and repent. Forgive me, restore me, and help me start again. In Jesus' name. Amen.

Seasons Change

So Naomi returned from Moab accompanied
by Ruth the Moabitess, her daughter-in-law, arriving
in Bethlehem as the barley harvest was beginning.

RUTH 1:22

When we're ready to return to God's chosen path for us, He won't make us walk there alone. He'll send reinforcements to help us on our journey. Sometimes He selects the unlikeliest of companions, but He knows what we need and will not leave us comfortless.

Ruth and Naomi had been struggling for a long time. Naomi said that she went away from home full and came back empty. She went away with a husband and sons and came back a childless widow. Now her season of life was changing. Harvest time had come. Life is seasonal. Today will not always be. Our circumstances will change. There will be ebbs and flows in fortune. But through all the ups and downs, God remains faithful. He will not leave us empty. At times, His correction may feel like a wound, but you'll feel His healing touch. And with the healing comes renewed strength.

In each change of season, discover the new fruit being produced. How is it manifesting in your life and in the lives of those around you? An old adage is "What doesn't kill you makes you stronger." This is so true...but only if we allow it to.

What season of life are you presently in? In what areas have you been depleted? How can you be refilled?

Dear heavenly Father, help me recognize the purpose for each season in my life. I want to be fruitful for You. In Jesus' name. Amen.

Starting Where You Are

So [Ruth] went out and began to glean in the fields behind the
harvesters. As it turned out, she found herself working in a field
belonging to Boaz, who was from the clan of Elimelech.

RUTH 2:3

The New King James Version says Ruth "happened" upon a field
belonging to Boaz. She found favor in his eyes. God's Word clearly
tells us the steps of the righteous are ordered by the Lord. That our days were
written in God's book before we were formed in the womb. Though Ruth
was a Moabite, a people despised by the Israelites, her story clearly shows us
that everyone, regardless of background or mistakes, can be redeemed and
crowned with favor. Perhaps it was Ruth's solid commitment to forsake the
ways of her people and embrace the God of Israel (Ruth 1:16). Perhaps it
was her commitment to care for her mother-in-law. Perhaps it was her willingness to humble herself and not despise being a servant. Better yet, I dare
say it was the accumulation of all these things that caught the heart of God
and the eye of Boaz. When we choose to work joyously with what we have
and glean from what is before us and available today, our tomorrows take
on momentum that helps us go where we wanted to be in the first place.
We can't see the entire picture of how our lives will unfold, but we can certainly start with where we are.

What can you do today to feed your spirit and serve others? What fields
are available to you? How willing are you to begin where you are and leave
the rest for God to unfold?

---

*Dear heavenly Father, show me where to begin. Lead me to
the center of Your purpose for me. In Jesus' name. Amen.*

How to Get Noticed

Just then Boaz arrived from Bethlehem and greeted
the harvesters, "The LORD be with you!" "The LORD bless you!"
they called back. Boaz asked the foreman of his harvesters,
"Whose young woman is that?"
RUTH 2:4-5

*I*f you want to be noticed just keep doing what you're doing—if it's the right thing...what God wants you to be doing. What did Ruth look like as she gleaned in the field? Maybe her long hair was tied in a scarf. Her clothing was probably conducive for working...not exactly beauty pageant material. And yet this man, Boaz, notices her...hmmm.

Perhaps a lot of us are trying too hard to catch men's attention. Consider this: It's not so much *how* we look, but *what we are doing* that will catch the eye of the man who is right for each of us. The truth still stands that he who finds a wife finds a good thing and obtains favor from the Lord (Proverbs 18:22). This removes a huge weight from women. We don't have to do the looking. We are prizes to be found! In the meantime, we get busy fulfilling the purposes God has called us to so we'll be in position to meet our future partners. That meeting will be on all the levels that count. Not just physical attraction but purpose, common interests, and other skills and traits that last a lifetime. So let's make every encounter and every activity count for something God can bless. After all, we never know who may be watching!

What are you focused on right now? Does your present focus bless or serve anyone?

Dear heavenly Father, order my steps that I may help those You want me to. Lead me toward the blessing You have for me. In Jesus' name. Amen.

Recognizing the Right One

So Boaz said to Ruth, "My daughter, listen to me. Don't go and glean in another field and don't go away from here. Stay here with my servant girls. Watch the field where the men are harvesting, and follow along after the girls. I have told the men not to touch you. And whenever you are thirsty, go and get a drink from the water jars the men have filled."

RUTH 2:8-9

*W*hat does Boaz look like? He is an intentional man who understands his role as a man of God. He knows what he wants. He has a sound reputation among his peers and coworkers. He moves effortlessly into his role as protector and provider. He is a brother in God who is sensitive to the needs of a woman without being overpowering. He sees a need and fills it without being asked. He is respectful. He doesn't presume anything, yet he looks to do what is within his power to help Ruth. Boaz is a man modeled after Christ, who has promised to lead us to green pastures and grant us rest, provision, and protection. Boaz is a man in harvest. He is fruitful and respected. He respected Ruth enough not to assume she would stay in his fields. He asked her to stay to ensure her safety.

Recently I watched a movie where the female lead was noting all the "signs" that reveal if the man in question liked her. Boaz models those signs! If none of this is happening in your life, especially if you're in a relationship, feel free to glean in other fields.

In what way is Christ the model of the man you want in your life? How can you set healthy standards in lieu of unrealistic expectations?

Dear heavenly Father, grant me the discernment to recognize the one You have for me. Give me the wisdom and strength not to settle for less than Your best for me. In Jesus' name. Amen.

Motives

At this, [Ruth] bowed down with her face to the ground.
She exclaimed, "Why have I found such favor in your eyes
that you notice me—a foreigner?" Boaz replied, "I've been told
all about what you have done for your mother-in-law since the
death of your husband—how you left your father and mother and
your homeland and came to live with a people you did not know
before. May the LORD repay you for what you have done."

RUTH 2:10-12

Our reputations will go before us and, as I've said before, we never know who is watching! As we do everything as unto the Lord in secret, God will reward us openly. Just when we feel no one has noticed what we've been doing, people invariably let us know they've been taking note. Just as we feel taken for granted, someone we weren't aware was observing us celebrates our contribution. God is like that.

Lest we get focused on one person's gratitude, praise will come from unanticipated sources. This I've learned. Until my motive is only that of doing what pleases God, I will get disgruntled with others often. There will never be enough gratitude displayed or praise given for my efforts. But as I do things to bless the heart of God, others respond to what I've done. Truly God repays! He draws close to those who humble themselves and resists those who are proud of their accomplishments. If you praise yourself, do you need any more praise? Your works should speak for you and reveal who you are. In this light of love and care and humility, we're magnets to those who seek happiness and fulfillment.

What is your attitude in giving and serving others? What is your motivation for what you do? When others aren't appreciative, how do you respond?

Dear heavenly Father, help me find joy in serving, knowing I'm bringing pleasure to Your heart. In Jesus' name. Amen.

Beauty Secrets

Wash and perfume yourself, and put on your best clothes.
RUTH 3:3

*T*he work of preparing for relationships is never done. We must constantly cleanse ourselves of wrong attitudes and thoughts and allow the Holy Spirit to perfume us with His fruit. As we enfold ourselves in garments of salvation, we are beautified by God and granted favor in the eyes of those around us. Many make the mistake of thinking that outward beauty is enough to get a man, keep a man, and get the love they're looking for. Then they wonder how someone they don't consider attractive managed to find an adoring mate. The answer? She's spent more time making that man feel needed and adored than calling attention to herself. This can only happen when we get over ourselves and value others as much, if not more, than ourselves.

Naomi's instructions to Ruth to wash and perfume herself was so she'd be prepared to go and see Boaz. Even though our goal is that our inner beauty will outshine our outer beauty, it doesn't hurt to be neat and presentable. True beauty comes from our spirits and shines forth as we're being modest, well-groomed, and constantly uplifting others.

In what ways do you make others feel celebrated and beautiful? What is your attitude toward men? How can you settle the issues that prolong any negative attitudes you have?

Dear heavenly Father, wash me, cleanse me, and beautify me with Your loveliness. In Jesus' name. Amen.

The Way to a Man's Heart

[Naomi told Ruth,] "Then go down to the threshing floor,
but don't let him know you are there until he has finished
eating and drinking. When he lies down, note the place where
he is lying. Then go and uncover his feet and lie down.
He will tell you what to do."

RUTH 3:3

There comes a time in every man's life, when the stage is set for him to feel ready for a mate. At the end of the harvest when he's had the opportunity to be fruitful, to separate what is needed in his life from what is not, to enter a place of rest about who he is as a man and where he is going in life. Take note, my sisters! Don't press your case for marriage before a man is ready. When he says he isn't ready, believe him. Allow him to get himself together and get into the right position. Only then will he consider making a decision about a mate. If you don't listen and continue on, you aren't honoring what he's saying. And you'll never be able to submit to a man you don't respect.

After Boaz had finished threshing his harvest, he was at rest and in the right position to become a husband. Remember, it was after Adam was at rest that Eve was fashioned for him. Boaz had settled his business, and that left room for Ruth to lay at his feet and put herself in a position to be covered by him. If we can't trust men to cover and lead us, they are not the men for us!

Are you at rest concerning your potential mate? Do you trust God with His timing for you coming together with the one He has chosen for you?

Dear heavenly Father, I give my heart back to You and ask You to keep it until the day You choose to present me to my mate. Prepare my heart to receive him, and prepare his heart to receive me. In Jesus' name. Amen.

The Heart of a Servant

"Who are you?" he asked. "I am your servant Ruth," she said.
"Spread the corner of your garment over me,
since you are a kinsman-redeemer."

RUTH 3:9

This conversation is deeper than it appears. Every man asks the woman he is considering, "Who are you?" And we must know the answer. Who do you want to be in the life of your potential mate? In the lives of those who matter to you? Who do you want to be to God?

The world has made "servant" a bad word, suggesting there is no honor in serving. However, service is a high calling and privilege. To serve our potential mates, our loved ones, and God is to live a life of fulfillment and lasting significance. As we serve others in Jesus' name, we find ourselves in the position to receive what God has for us.

We all need a redeemer at various turns in our lives—a covering, a provider, a protector. All of these are ensured by God as we walk before Him and others with a servant heart. Joyfully giving of ourselves begins a delightful cycle of giving and reciprocation. Until we can joyfully say, "I am your servant," true fulfillment will elude us.

Who are you? Who has God placed in your life for you to serve? In what ways do you need God to cover and redeem you?

———————————— �֎ ————————————

Dear heavenly Father, as I pour myself out in service to others, cover and keep me. In Jesus' name. Amen.

Unexpected Blessing

"The LORD bless you, my daughter," [Boaz replied to Ruth].
"This kindness is greater than that which you showed earlier:
You have not run after the younger men, whether rich or poor."
RUTH 3:10

One of a man's greatest fears is rejection, but perhaps an even more pressing question in his mind is whether he is your preference. What if he is not physically your type? Or the kind of man you were originally looking for? Part of his identity is wrapped up in what he does and how he is seen in the eyes of the woman he loves.

Boaz felt blessed that Ruth had approached him about being her kinsman-redeemer. Although this move was dictated by tradition in the region at that time, Ruth was not bound to Jewish tradition because she was from Moab. In his mind she could have offered herself to a host of other men that she found more to her liking. He must have found her beautiful and thought he might be too old for her. Yet here she was at his feet, willing to submit to his leadership should he choose to step up to the role.

Sometimes we get so stuck on a "type" of man that we fail to see the blessing standing before us. A different package distracts us from the wonderful contents that could be awaiting us in someone. Perhaps it's time to look again?

What characteristics do you want in your mate? Have you overlooked these in others based on their external qualities?

Dear heavenly Father, help me look past the surface to see the true riches in the hearts of others. In Jesus' name. Amen.

The End of the Matter

Then Naomi said, "Wait, my daughter, until you find out what happens. For the man will not rest until the matter is settled today."
RUTH 3:18

A man who knows what he wants will pursue his choice. If he wants you, he'll find a way to make you his. He will not rest until the matter is settled. God has placed something in the spirit of a man that sounds the alarm when he sees "the one." Until then he may allow himself to be chosen by others, but when he sees that special woman he will move heaven and earth to claim her as his bride. When a man loves a woman, he'll do whatever he has to do to win his prize.

This is the model set by Jesus Christ, who is the ultimate Bridegroom. Jesus pursued, wooed, fought for, and died for His bride. And His bride wasn't even aware of who He was! She was willful, skeptical, and unresponsive, but Jesus did not and still has not given up on her. And so we wait for the day when He comes back to claim His beloved—us and everyone who accepts Jesus as Lord and Savior! And He will not rest until the matter is settled.

What are you waiting for? How do you imagine Jesus feels as He waits for you to join Him in heaven?

Dear heavenly Father, as we anticipate the day I will finally be with You in heaven, teach me how to love You even more. In Jesus' name. Amen.

Paying the Price

Then Boaz said, "On the day you buy the land from Naomi and
from Ruth the Moabitess, you acquire the dead man's widow,
in order to maintain the name of the dead with his property."
At this, the kinsman-redeemer said, "Then I cannot
redeem it because I might endanger my own estate.
You redeem it yourself. I cannot do it."

RUTH 4:5-6

What we must understand as women is that not every man is going to be willing to pay the price to be with us. Love is a decision of great sacrifice. Boaz knew that another cousin in the family tree was in line before him for the hand of Ruth. He also knew that most men are interested in the benefits but not necessarily the responsibility and price of relationship. This cousin was interested in acquiring the field that came with Ruth. He wasn't willing to redeem her to get the field because it would cost him and put his own holdings in danger because any offspring between them would inherit some of his wealth.

When it comes to us, Jesus thought it well worth it to leave heaven and come to earth to live in lowly estate to the point of death for us. He made the greatest sacrifice for our sake. His love for us was—and is!—so great. That's some kind of love!

What are you willing to sacrifice for the sake of the one you love?

———————————— ✠ ————————————

*Dear heavenly Father, help me be a blessing just as much as
I seek to be blessed. In Jesus' name. Amen.*

A Match Made in Heaven

So Boaz took Ruth and she became his wife.
Then he went to her, and the LORD enabled her
to conceive, and she gave birth to a son.

RUTH 4:13

Boaz closed the deal. Ruth had to do nothing but wait. As Ruth waited, Boaz did what was needed to be done to secure Ruth as his wife. In spite of Ruth's background, she was given a place of honor. Perhaps Boaz had been prepared for her long ago. His mother was Rahab, the harlot who helped Joshua's spies in Jericho. He was well acquainted with the difficulties of being a foreigner and an outcast. Boaz and Ruth were a match made in heaven.

When we wait for God's perfect timing in our lives, all things come together and work for our good. The signature of God on anything we do in life is fruitfulness. Every good and perfect gift comes from God and bears fruit. And that fruit blesses us and those around us. God gives us the ability by His Spirit to not only produce good works but also fruit that lasts. Every relationship we have should be greater than the two people involved. When God puts two people together, they've been divinely prepared for one another to become a marvelous manifestation of God's purposes. In Boaz and Ruth's situation, God was glorified and others were blessed. Sounds like a power couple to me!

Why do you want to get married? What would you like your marriage to produce in the lives of others?

———————————— �֍ ————————————

Dear heavenly Father, prepare me for the one You have for me as You prepare him for me. I want both of us to be a marvelous reflection of Your love and blessing. In Jesus' name. Amen.

The media is filled with shows and movies depicting various ways to find or be chosen by the men of our dreams. These have caused some people to follow their lead and experience disappointment and heartache. Is there a divine design for dating, mating, and relating? Yes. The outline is very clear in Scripture through stories told of "how to be found." Some themes repeat, forming a picture of the spiritual protocol for coming together. How interesting that so many accounts detail that a woman was found or chosen because she was at a well getting water or serving someone or being set apart in some way.

In the story of Esther, the scenario is a bit different, but once again, she was chosen...chosen from among a bevy of beauties. Think of it as an ancient version of our modern-day *Bachelorette*. Keep in mind, however, that Esther didn't volunteer to be in the competition. And she chose to do things differently from the others. Let's see what we can learn about truly being set apart.

The Right Response

On the seventh day, when King Xerxes was in high spirits
from wine, he commanded the seven eunuchs who served him...
to bring before him Queen Vashti, wearing her royal crown,
in order to display her beauty to the people and nobles, for
she was lovely to look at. But when the attendants delivered
the king's command, Queen Vashti refused to come.
Then the king became furious and burned with anger.

ESTHER 1:10-12

No relationship should ever be taken for granted. Sometimes when we choose to stand on principle, we find ourselves standing alone. The general understanding is that King Xerxes was making an unreasonable request of Vashti because he'd been drinking. So perhaps Vashti was reasonably hesitant to parade herself in front of the inebriated crowd. But stepping outside that situation, let's consider relationships in general.

We need to be careful how we respond to others, especially when other people are present and watching. There is a way to be right without creating more wrong. All of our relationships, from intimate to platonic, need to reflect "relationship" from heaven's point of view. What is this? Love that is patient, gracious, and understanding. Every challenge we face in relationships is another way to show how God would have us respond rather than our human nature reacting. Anytime we respond in anger, fear, or pride, we may say or do the wrong thing and exacerbate the situation. We are to pursue peace above all things. Peace is the preamble to joy and the foundation to enduring love.

When you're asked to do things that go against your values or views, how do you respond? Is there a gracious way to keep your standards without the other person feeling slighted or humiliated?

---

*Dear heavenly Father, help me be gracious in my responses
to others. In Jesus' name. Amen.*

The Power of Influence

Then Memucan replied in the presence of the king and the nobles,
"Queen Vashti has done wrong, not only against the king but also
against all the nobles and the peoples of all the provinces of King
Xerxes. For the queen's conduct will become known to all the
women, and so they will despise their husbands and say,
'King Xerxes commanded Queen Vashti to be brought before him,
but she would not come.' This very day the Persian and Median
women of the nobility who have heard about the queen's conduct
will respond to all the king's nobles in the same way.
There will be no end of disrespect and discord."

ESTHER 1:16-18

What goes on at your house affects the kingdom at large. We are called to be an influence for good. Why? Because others are looking and making heavenly judgments in light of our earthly actions. The Word says the Lord leads us in paths of righteousness for *His name's sake*. We affect God's reputation. We set the standard for how others see God. Our standards and behaviors affect the actions and choices of others.

The apostle Paul said a little yeast leavens the whole lump. A biblical proverb says bad companions corrupt good manners. I'm sure we are all aware that what we do affects others, but sometimes we don't understand how far it goes. People may decide to do the right thing or wrong thing based on our actions. Our influence is more powerful than we realize.

Who have been your greatest influencers? What type of influence are you for others?

———————————— ✢ ————————————

Dear heavenly Father, help me make every decision in light of eternity and Your reputation. In Jesus' name. Amen.

The Cost of Offense

*Therefore, if it pleases the king, let him issue a royal decree
and let it be written in the laws of Persia and Media, which
cannot be repealed, that Vashti is never again to enter the
presence of King Xerxes. Also let the king give her royal position
to someone else who is better than she. Then when the king's
edict is proclaimed throughout all his vast realm, all the women
will respect their husbands, from the least to the greatest.*

ESTHER 1:19-20

There is no such thing as being indispensible. In the book of Proverbs it says that when the king smiles there is favor. Ah, but when the king is offended, he becomes a brother that is stronger than a fortified city. When possible, offense is to be avoided because it gives birth to no good thing and can attract great losses. Sometimes permanent damage can be done to relationships and lives can be scarred forever. In some instances there can be no turning back, especially if the offense was a public one. Then pride becomes the nail in the coffin as many feel the sting of shame more sharply than the pain of the original offense.

How can we avoid offending someone when a request is unreasonable? Proverbs 15:1 says, "A gentle answer turns away wrath."

People watch to see how we will respond to life issues. Often they draw conclusions that color their own behaviors. So let's be careful about our choices and how we respond to others whether we agree or not with what's being asked.

When you are offended, how do you respond to the one who offended you? How difficult is it to mend relationships that have been broken? How can God's grace be applied to the situation?

Dear heavenly Father, help me be sensitive to the needs of others. Grant me the grace to seek reconciliation if I offend someone. In Jesus' name. Amen.

New Beginnings

Then the king's personal attendants proposed, "Let a search be made for beautiful young virgins for the king."
ESTHER 2:2

As hard as it may be to conceive of in the midst of these liberal times, every man is still looking for the woman who is a "private garden, a spring that no one else can have, a fountain of my own" as King Solomon proudly cited about his bride (Song of Songs 4:12 TLB). I realize that not every unmarried woman is a virgin, but God is able to restore our virginity as we give our bodies to Him and repent of the choices we made.

But an even greater issue goes beyond the physical to our heart conditions. One of the items listed under the virtuous woman's description in Proverbs 31 was the fact that her husband's heart trusted in her. A woman pure of heart is great assurance to a man. He wants to know that his woman's heart toward him is genuine. He doesn't want to fear manipulation or deceit from her. He doesn't want to sleep with the enemy. This is why it is important to allow God to heal our hearts from past relationships. We want to be free from the baggage of past encounters and disappointments. No one wants to pay for the last bad experience you had.

In light of this revelation, search your heart. Give your past to God and allow Him to give you a new start. He'll cleanse you and restore you. Then get ready to be found!

What are you holding on to from the past that will affect your future relationships? What do you need to let go of to embrace a new start?

Dear heavenly Father, restore my heart and make me new. In Jesus' name. Amen.

The Set-apart Life

Many girls were brought to the citadel of Susa and put under the care of Hegai. Esther also was taken to the king's palace and entrusted to Hegai, who had charge of the harem. The girl pleased him and won his favor. Immediately he provided her with her beauty treatments and special food. He assigned to her seven maids selected from the king's palace and moved her and her maids into the best place in the harem.

ESTHER 2:8-9

There is something to be said for being set apart. Trust me, the place God has called us to is not a common thoroughfare. Everyone doesn't answer the call to make the sacrifices needed to accomplish great things through Jesus Christ. As princesses in our heavenly King's court, our lives will change. We don't want to go where we used to go or eat what we used to eat if they go against God's standards. Where we go, what we do, and what we digest or ingest becomes part of us. What we have constantly before our eyes will affect our mindsets, attitudes, and actions, just as those we choose as our companions influence us for good or bad. God has called us away from "the usual" to a higher calling, a greater life that will often go against the grain of where most people live. He has a special beauty regime for us. In God's kingdom and service, there is no place for mediocrity or substandard living.

In what ways can you challenge yourself to a greater level of living in Christ?

———————————— ✛ ————————————

Dear heavenly Father, help me embrace being set apart, knowing it is for my good and Your glory. In Jesus' name. Amen.

The Right Beauty Regimen

Before a girl's turn came to go in to King Xerxes, she had to
complete twelve months of beauty treatments prescribed
for the women, six months with oil of myrrh
and six with perfumes and cosmetics.

ESTHER 2:12

There is a time of preparation for every level of life we allow God
to complete in us. There are some things He wants to establish
in us. We can consider ourselves buildings that are being upgraded. Some
parts have to be leveled. Some torn up. Some tossed out to make room for
something new and more glorious. We die to the things we've grown used to
and perhaps held dear to make room for the new in Christ! Yes, this dying
to self can be painful, but it will surely lead to new lives that will be above
and beyond our expectations!

Once we've surrendered to God and allowed Him to clear away all that
is not conducive to moving forward and being fruitful in Him, the decorat-
ing and sweetening begins. And that's when the fragrance of a surrendered
and beautified life begins to have an intoxicating effect on those around us.
This process is necessary if we are to grow and mature into who God wants
us to be—godly, *desirable* women.

When we walk in love and give off the aroma of the fruit of the Spirit,
we glorify and please God and bless others. God is passionate about beau-
tifying us for His name's sake. How long does the process take? As long
as necessary. Let's joyfully submit to it and cling to the truth that God is
doing a great work in us.

What areas do you feel God is working out in your life right now? What
has been the process for your beautification?

———————————— ✠ ————————————

Dear heavenly Father, I submit to Your will and to Your way.
Beautify me and saturate me with Your Spirit. In Jesus' name.
Amen.

Beauty Secrets

When the turn came for Esther (the girl Mordecai had adopted,
the daughter of his uncle Abihail) to go to the king, she asked
for nothing other than what Hegai, the king's eunuch
who was in charge of the harem, suggested.

ESTHER 2:15

We depend on so many external things to attract the love we're looking for, but after everything else is stripped away what is inside is all that counts. In the mad rush of competition to catch the eye of available men, the outside of the package can become overrated. Yes, it's true that we must first catch the eye of a man, but if what we have to offer doesn't capture his heart, the attraction will be short-lived. This calls for a special sensitivity in our spirits to knowing and understanding the needs of the men around us. Remember that we have been created to not just be "help meets" to our mates but also blessings and gifts.

What we have to give in relationships is more important than what we will get out of them. In light of this, after all the primping and dressing is over, if we haven't paid more attention to our spirits and our wholeness in Christ, we may end up being just another woman in a harem (figuratively speaking, or course!). So what will separate us from the rest of the pack? What God has placed inside us!

What do you rely on to attract attention from others? And from men specifically? What do you need to develop to be more of a blessing to others?

───────────────── �֍ ─────────────────

Dear heavenly Father, transform me from within into a beautiful reflection of Your love and glory. In Jesus' name. Amen.

The Ultimate Bridegroom

Now the king was attracted to Esther more than to any of
the other women, and she won his favor and approval more than
any of the other virgins. So he set a royal crown on her head
and made her queen instead of Vashti. And the king gave
a great banquet, Esther's banquet, for all his nobles and officials.
He proclaimed a holiday throughout the provinces
and distributed gifts with royal liberality.

ESTHER 2:17-18

In the film *He's Just Not That into You,* the hero of the story is quick to tell the heroine that the true sign of a man's attraction and affection is that he moves in to close the deal. This is true. He will forsake all others to crown his woman queen when she captures his heart. Until then, a woman should never assume she is "the one." When this is settled in a man's heart, he goes all out to celebrate the love he's found.

God created us to be celebrated over by the ones He presents us to. When we look at our lists of what we want in a man, we should be sure to separate fairy-tale expectations from God's standards and preferences for us. If we have to wonder about a man's intentions or his love for us, the answer is clear. Many times we don't want to receive that the men we're seeing are not the ones for us, but being careful and clear is the best prevention to getting into a wrong relationship that will turn out disastrous. God celebrates and dances over us—and our life partners should too.

What are your expectations for your mate in light of Jesus' example as the ultimate Bridegroom?

———————————— ❊ ————————————

Dear heavenly Father, secure my heart in You. Fill me so that I won't settle for less than what You've chosen for me. In Jesus' name. Amen.

Divine Connections

Mordecai told [Esther's servant Hathach] everything that had happened to him, including the exact amount of money Haman had promised to pay into the royal treasury for the destruction of the Jews. He also gave him a copy of the text of the edict...to show to Esther and explain it to her, and he told him to urge her to go into the king's presence to beg for mercy and plead with him for her people.

Esther 4:7-8

"And who knows but that you have come to royal position for such a time as this?"

Esther 4:14

God strategically aligns our relationships for more than our personal pleasure. Who can say what Esther's reaction was to being chosen to be queen? Perhaps she sat in awe of her good fortune thinking, *Fancy that!* Perhaps she was scared. The true purposes for all the divine connections will be realized in due season. This is when we find out we've been preselected according to God's purposes to be where we are.

We can miss His goals for us if we only focus on our viewpoint. We are all bridges to the lives God has created us all to live. There will be seasons of intercession, of walking together, of standing "in the gap" for one another, of bearing one another's infirmities. Marriage magnifies all of this and takes it to another level. As women we will be major influences in our men's lives. We can either prayerfully exhort them toward their purpose in Christ or not. What we do will affect them and others in and beyond our immediate sphere of influence.

Why do you want to be married? What will you contribute to the life of the man God will place you with? What do you expect in return?

Dear heavenly Father, help me be open and discerning about the purpose for every relationship You have blessed me with. In Jesus' name. Amen.

There are times in our lives when we conclude that we have weathered so many storms and emotional disappointments that we want to resign from the healthy space of expecting from God. We become apathetic and emotionally paralyzed, preferring not to feel anything or anticipate anything lest we be disappointed again. This is exactly where the enemy of our souls would like us to be. In this space we can lose sight of the faithfulness of God and miss His blessings. We can become so jaded we wouldn't recognize the blessings if they walked up and slapped us.

But thankfully God is faithful to meet us on the road of inward mourning. He will give us the strength to lift our chins and face the challenges of life. We rededicate ourselves to Him and choose to believe again...to receive what He has prepared and has waiting for us—rivers of refreshing for our hearts and souls.

The Battle for Self-worth

When a Samaritan woman came to draw water, Jesus said to her,
"Will you give me a drink?" (His disciples had gone into the town
to buy food.) The Samaritan woman said to him, "You are
a Jew and I am a Samaritan woman. How can you ask me
for a drink?" (For Jews do not associate with Samaritans.)

JOHN 4:7-9

*H*ow we see ourselves colors our expectations and sets us up to sometimes attract the very things we don't want. The Samaritan woman at the well had obviously died by degrees, burrowing deeper and deeper into self-hatred and resignation. This is how we sometimes miss the very blessings God has reserved for us.

I'm the wrong gender, wrong race, wrong religion, wrong everything! That's what this woman in today's verse was thinking. Yet none of this information had been solicited from Jesus. He simply asked her for a drink of water. Perhaps when someone just says hello, we shouldn't look beyond the greeting and assume what their intentions are. Maybe we need to take the moment at face value. This will occur more easily and more often when we are whole and secure in who God has made us to be.

But when we see ourselves as broken, with shattered pieces of our hearts scattered all over, we worry they'll reveal themselves at the most inopportune times and sabotage our blessings. We are worthy of more than we know through Christ's great sacrifice and love!

In what ways have you sabotaged blessings and relationships in the past? In what ways do you underestimate your worth?

Dear heavenly Father, mend my heart and help me see me through Your eyes so I'll recognize my true worth. In Jesus' name. Amen.

If Only We Knew

Jesus answered her, "If you knew the gift of God
and who it is that asks you for a drink, you would have
asked him and he would have given you living water."

JOHN 4:10

Life is not all about us. God is bigger than all our fears and alleged shortcomings. We need to take our focus off us and put it where the solution lies. Before we approached God, He had our files. He knew everything about us already and had moved past it. He wasn't looking at where we were or where we were going.

God looks forward to what He knows we will become. The details of all we lack isn't what captures His interest. He is too excited about what His Spirit can achieve in us. If only we knew what God knew about us! If we knew what He sees in our futures, our focus would be different, more upbeat. Our prayers would be more dynamic and frequent.

Let's stop spending time nursing and rehearsing our problems. Instead, we can focus on the One who is Lord over all the problems and hindrances in our lives. He is waiting to give us all the things He knows we long for—blessings alive with the promise of more to come.

What have you been asking God for? What needs to change about your requests?

———————————— ✠ ————————————

Dear heavenly Father, my cup is empty. Fill me with You. In Jesus' name. Amen.

The Danger of Disappointment

"Sir," the woman said, "you have nothing to draw with and the well is deep. Where can you get this living water? Are you greater than our father Jacob, who gave us the well and drank from it himself, as did also his sons and his flocks and herds?"

JOHN 4:11-12

When we've grown weary from disappointment, it's hard to have hope that anything different can occur. When others come offering solutions, we're apt to swat away their suggestions before they've even finished their sentences. *My issues are deep, and you are not equipped to deal with what I'm going through,* we think. *As a matter of fact, no one has been able to help me in my situation. What makes you think you have anything to offer?* If we're truly honest, our futile efforts to control something in our world is what makes us refuse to move forward and possibly face further disappointment. Alas, the irony is this never works. Hope is so powerful. We need to keep it alive! We need to refuse the lie of the enemy that things will never be different. God says we have hope in Him. All we've suffered will be used by Him to help us grow.

How can we handle what we're going through? Adjust our expectations. Don't focus on "the well," focus on the One who gives us living water! In other words, concentrate on what stands before us now—new opportunities for joy.

What disappointments have caused you to forfeit faith? What do you need to do to reclaim hopeful expectations?

———————————————— ✠ ————————————————

Dear heavenly Father, help my unbelief. In Jesus' name I pray. Amen.

True Satisfaction

Jesus answered, "Everyone who drinks this water
will be thirsty again, but whoever drinks the water I give him
will never thirst. Indeed, the water I give him will become
in him a spring of water welling up to eternal life."

JOHN 4:13-14

"Empty calories." We've all heard this when dealing with diets. Empty calories fill us up but profit us nothing. They offer little or no nutrition and cause our hunger to return in short measure. Such is life in many areas. We have a tendency to get lured into temporary gratification, which almost always leaves us hungering for more.

How many times have we dated someone we knew wasn't "the one" we were looking for, which created more drama as time went on and conflicts arose. Time and time again we fall into this trap. For some people the problem is shopaholism or feeding sorrow with food. There are so many ways we try to fill the empty space within but still come up empty.

God basically asks, "Why do you spend money and time on what doesn't fill or satisfy? Come to Me and eat what is good! Let your soul delight in healthy nutrition!" There is a place of abiding satisfaction that does not wane. It's not found in earthly pleasures or people. It's only in the secret place where God meets us and renews us. That is perpetual fulfillment!

Feeling hungry? Check your food source. What things offer temporary gratification to you? In what ways do you lack the satisfaction you're looking for?

———————— ✠ ————————

Dear heavenly Father, give me a discerning eye for what really satisfies. In Jesus' name. Amen.

Breaking the Cycle

The woman said to him, "Sir, give me this water so that I won't get thirsty and have to keep coming here to draw water."
JOHN 4:15

Don't you long to break the negative cycles in your life? To be free of repeat scenarios that bring discomfort and pain? Of course!

Like the woman at the well, we welcome the thought of a new adventure, of another level of living where we get past the things that keep bogging us down. Cycles of loss and heartbreak, failure in businesses or relationships happen over and over again. *What does it take to break free?* we wonder. *I can't believe I'm back at the same place again. It's frustrating!* Sometimes we feel like crawling out of our skins. We don't want to be who we are and want what we want. The Lord stands ready, waiting to show us what is at the root of the desire that drives us to the same destination again and again. The yearning is only the fruit of the branch. God wants to get to the roots so He can help us settle the problem once and for all. He is waiting to set us free. All we need to do is be open to the truth and the wholeness God holds in store.

What is the repeat cycle in your life? What drives you to the same point again and again?

Dear heavenly Father, break this negative cycle in my life. Grant me a new start. In Jesus' name. Amen.

Facing the Truth

[Jesus] told her, "Go, call your husband and come back."
"I have no husband," she replied. Jesus said to her, "You are right
when you say you have no husband. The fact is, you have had five
husbands, and the man you now have is not your husband.
What you have just said is quite true."

JOHN 4:16-18

God is deliberate in the way He pushes our buttons and forces us to deal with the things we want to avoid. In His way He guides us to the truth. When we are willing to submit everything in our situation to Him we can wrap that issue up and move on together as partners. God won't fix what we don't ask Him to. He is a gentleman. He will not intrude on our personal space. He waits to be invited to help. And when He comes, He brings His healing and deliverance. He doesn't judge where we've been, but speaks the truth in love to get us in right standing with Him. He corrects, restores, and encourages us to choose Him and to follow His instructions.

The woman at the well was caught up in a cycle of relationships that didn't work out for one reason or another. And she had probably vowed to not allow herself to be hurt anymore. This time she would take control and not invest in a commitment. She wouldn't get married; she would merely live with a man. Yet she was more lonely and isolated than ever. And now Jesus was showing that He knew all about her...all about the bad choices and current situation. And yet He still longed to help her. Yes, restoration begins with the truth.

What truths have you been avoiding? What vows have you made to protect your heart?

Dear heavenly Father, I lay down my defenses and give You my heart to restore and keep safe. In Jesus' name. Amen.

True Worship

Jesus declared, "Believe me, woman, a time is coming
when you will worship the Father neither on this mountain nor in
Jerusalem…A time is coming and has now come when the true
worshipers will worship the Father in spirit and truth, for they are
the kind of worshipers the Father seeks. God is spirit, and
his worshipers must worship in spirit and in truth."

JOHN 4:21,23-24

*I*t's one thing to know the truth; it's another to embrace it and let it set us free. What are we worshiping today? Is marriage the idol on the mantle of our hearts? It must be replaced by God. He is looking for worshipers. True worship is surrendering all we are and all we have so God can do with us as He pleases. Worship isn't just lifting our hands and singing songs of praise. We need to surrender our lives to Him. We need to walk out that surrender in obedience. As we do, God fills us to overflowing and satisfies our greatest hunger.

The woman at the well was looking for something that would satisfy her inner craving. Men hadn't done it. Following the rules of her religion hadn't done it. She was still thirsty and searching for more…of what she didn't know. But when she finally laid her life at the feet of Jesus, she realized what she was looking for all along was her Messiah. And this is true for all of us.

What have you been worshiping? What "truth" do you need to replace with God's truth? What areas do you need to surrender to God?

Dear heavenly Father, I surrender all that I am and desire to You. I choose to worship You in spirit and in truth. In Jesus' name. Amen.

Contagious!

Then, leaving her water jar, the woman went back to
the town and said to the people, "Come, see a man
who told me everything I ever did. Could this be the Christ?"
They came out of the town and made their way toward him.

JOHN 4:28-30

When the full revelation of who Jesus is becomes real to us, what we were seeking will no longer hold us captive. The woman at the well went seeking water but left without it because her encounter with Christ changed her quest. She no longer needed that water. She had found living water in her Lord. And her fulfillment was contagious. She was equipped to face her fears and those who had offended and misunderstood her. Those who shunned her followed her back to Jesus to encounter Him.

Because of the woman at the well's words, many people believed in Jesus. And when they heard Jesus for themselves, many more came to trust in Him. And the ones who believed by the woman's testimony became stronger in their belief after hearing Jesus.

This is where God wants all of us to be—so emptied of our desires and so entrenched in a life of worshiping Him that others see Christ in us without the filter of all we struggle with. As we shatter the idols in our hearts, Christ comes bearing gifts that replace them and make His glory more apparent in our lives.

What things or people do you need to let go of? What or whom do you need to face? In what ways can Christ become more visible in your life?

Dear heavenly Father, help me be such a living testimony of Your love and power that my love for You becomes contagious. In Jesus' name. Amen.

The Right Diet

Everything we do in life should feed us. Our worship of God should feed us. Obedience to God should feed us. Our other relationships and interactions should feed us. Our gifting and the way we bless others should feed us. Jesus came that we might have life and have it more abundantly. Everything we do should add to our lives. Then we can share this life and be blessed by being blessings to others.

When we walk in obedience to God, doing what He has called us to do, we are fed. We don't live by bread alone but by every word that proceeds from the mouth of God! God's instructions, encouragement, reminders of what is true, right, and worthy of praise feed and strengthen us for the journey of life and empower us to live unreservedly for Jesus.

What feeds you? What drains you? When you are focused on Jesus, what matters become less pressing?

Dear heavenly Father, for so long I've fed myself the wrong things. Help me find the nourishing, life-giving food You offer. In Jesus' name. Amen.

*A New Level
of Loving*

At times we can be our worst enemy. The things we blame God for are of our own making. As we submit to the influences around us, our faith may falter and we fail to make the choices that keep us where God wants us to be. In those moments, we need to own our bad choices and come clean with God.

Are you stuck in a never-ending cycle of dissatisfaction? What beliefs, attitudes, and habits contribute to that? Partner with God and submit to His timing so you'll be in position to receive what He wants to give: healing, deliverance, wholeness, peace, joy, and more love than you've ever known.

Self-examination can be hard because we don't necessarily like what we see, but it is needful if we want to get to another level of living and loving in Christ. It's time to break free of all that binds you and open your arms to receive what God has for you.

Birds of a Feather

*Now there is in Jerusalem near the Sheep Gate a pool,
which in Aramaic is called Bethesda and which is surrounded
by five covered colonnades. Here a great number of disabled
people used to lie—the blind, the lame, the paralyzed. One
who was there had been an invalid for thirty-eight years.*

JOHN 5:2-5

Birds of a feather flock together." Another adage is "Bad company corrupts good manners." And these are true. We will become the company we keep. People who gathered at the pool of Bethesda had suffering in common. I'm sure many sat day after day and commiserated about their aches and pains.

They were there because the pool was known for its healing properties. They probably speculated on when the angel would come to trouble the waters and wagered on who would get in first and get healed (John 5:4 NASB). Perhaps some were hopeful, but some had probably become jaded from being broken and rejected for a long time.

Can you relate to that? We've all been there, whether we were among a group of singles, folks who hated their jobs, or people who spent too much time watching bad news and concluding life is that way. We can settle for where we are based on the company we keep. We sink to the level of the "norm" around us. Perhaps it's time for new company and a new mindset.

Do you need to make an attitude adjustment? What is the common consensus of those in your inner circle? In what ways would you like your life to be different? Do you know anyone whose life looks that way?

Dear heavenly Father, change my mindset and transform my life. In Jesus' name. Amen.

Getting Honest

When Jesus saw him lying there and learned that
he had been in this condition for a long time,
he asked him, "Do you want to get well?"

JOHN 5:6

God seems to ask odd questions at times. But it wasn't so ridiculous after all. Some people don't really want to be well. They like the situation they're in because it gets them attention. Never mind that it's not positive attention—it's still getting noticed. Before moving on to wholeness, we need to be honest with ourselves. Many people *say* they want romantic relationships, yet in reality they are commitment phobes. Many profess to love men, but really they don't like them much.

Most of our unresolved issues evolve around inconsistencies in our hearts and minds. A house divided against itself can't stand. In fact, it will implode. People who say they want a relationship but haven't dealt with any serious past issues as well as significant inner conflicts will sabotage most encounters and forever be "the victims" without seeing their part in the demise of their relationships.

What is keeping you back from what you want out of life may very well be within you. God won't force you to confront anything you're not able to handle. But when it's time to move, God comes asking questions.

What do you want? How badly do you want it? What are you willing to sacrifice to have it?

---

*Dear heavenly Father, help my faltering heart. Make me whole
and prepare me to receive all You have for me. In Jesus' name.
Amen.*

No Excuses

"Sir," the invalid replied, "I have no one to help me
into the pool when the water is stirred. While I am trying
to get in, someone else goes down ahead of me."

JOHN 5:7

Always a bridesmaid never a bride. Sigh. I used to think everyone
else was getting what they wanted while I struggled and had to
wait patiently for results. Can you relate? The question Jesus asked the crippled man at the pool had nothing to do with the invalid's answer. Jesus
asked him if he wanted to be whole. His response was to give the reason
why he wasn't.

We all have excuses for why we do and don't do things, but in the end
are we telling the truth...or just the truth as we want to know it? How badly
do we want what we want?

If the disabled man really wanted to be whole, wouldn't he have positioned himself differently after 38 years? Tried a little harder? We don't know
the entire story, but somewhere along the way this man became resigned
to his lot. He lost hope. The enemy of our souls loves it when we drop the
faith ball. He knows if we shift our focus to what we're not or what we don't
have, we're sure to become undone. And that usually leads us to compare
ourselves to others, which is a battle no one can win. There will always be
someone more beautiful and smarter than us. But this has nothing to do
with what God has for us! We have no excuse for failure, for remaining
broken, because we have hope through Jesus Christ!

What is your excuse for not being where you want to be in life? Who
are you comparing yourself to in the midst of your struggles? How might
this affect the outcome?

---

*Dear heavenly Father, forgive me for making excuses. Help me
stop comparing myself to others and embrace Your strength
for the journey we're taking together. In Jesus' name. Amen.*

Renewing Your Mind

Then Jesus said to him, "Get up! Pick up your mat and walk."
At once the man was cured; he picked up his mat and walked.
JOHN 5:8-9

*W*hat is your excuse? Why not do away with everything that has kept you in your paralyzed state? You can take the time to reflect and even mourn, if necessary. But don't stay there! Healing and liberty await! Get up. Shake the dust off. Move.

Too often the only thing that stands between us and our healing (or anything else we desire) is a decision. We have the power in Christ to decide not to give in to what we see or experience. We can choose to see with eyes of faith. To know and trust that God is going to bring good out of every situation.

Our minds are so influential. We build mental "monuments" to support what we believe—whether it is true or not. Once it is established in our minds, our bodies follow our minds' instructions, and our paths are chosen. If our minds can lead us into bondage, can they also release us? Yes! A simple command from Jesus was all it took to get a man to rise to his feet and walk after 38 years of paralysis! The cure begins with obeying the command of Christ, no matter what we're thinking or experiencing.

Have you been believing any lies about yourself? What is keeping you from the life you want? What will shatter your paralysis? What steps to freedom can you take today?

————————————— ✻ —————————————

Heavenly Father, grant me the strength to respond to Your voice and take Your Word to heart. In Jesus' name. Amen.

Love that Sees

They came to Bethsaida, and some people brought
a blind man and begged Jesus to touch him.
MARK 8:22

In some cases we're unaware that we're blind, that we're not seeing what those around us see. This is why intercession and communication are so important. In those moments when we can't see our need for the Lord's intervention, we need to thank God for those who pray and carry us into His presence whether we want to go or not. The old saying "Love is blind" is a fallacy. Let me clarify that. The world's version of love may be blind, but God's love sees the needs of the ones He loves and finds solutions.

If we truly love, we will carry our loved ones and their concerns and lay them at the feet of Jesus. We will cover them in love with our prayers and understanding until they are whole once more. Yes, love stands with the ones who are broken, never abandoning, criticizing, or judging. It stands in the gap until the one being carried is able to stand on his or her own.

Who do you need to carry to Jesus in prayer? How have you handled this person's failure to see what you see? What type of responses have you gotten?

Dear heavenly Father, today I bring my friend before You. Please reach out to her with Your love and healing touch. In Jesus' name. Amen.

Moving Beyond the Pain

He took the blind man by the hand and led him outside the village.
MARK 8:23

*W*here we are can have a bearing on our condition and our blessing. There are times in our lives when we are so deeply entrenched in our situations that God has to take us by the hand and lead us beyond our normal boundaries so we can look back and see the forest for what it is…a group of individual trees. We need to take a step back and look at our last relationships. Remember not to romanticize it. See it as it was. The good, the bad, the ugly. What it cost. What was unaffordable.

So many times we're like the Israelites in the Old Testament. We're on our way to the promised land, but because we're not getting there when we think we should, we pine for what we had. We forget that we cried out to God to get us out of there. And now that we're not sure where we're going, maybe the last place wasn't so bad after all. That is the *illusion* that blindness paints. What was undesirable then is still undesirable—we just can't see it. When we embrace the clarity that comes from stepping outside of ourselves and where we formerly lived, we'll get a clearer view of the path that leads to healing and blessing.

What do you need to be painfully honest with yourself about? What has kept you clinging to a rose-colored vision of what isn't true? What do you fear if you face the truth?

———————————— ⁂ ————————————

Dear heavenly Father, I realize that the truth will set me free. Make a way of escape out of this trouble or help me bear it. In Jesus' name. Amen.

Getting the Right Perspective

When he had spit on the man's eyes and put his hands on him,
Jesus asked, "Do you see anything?" He looked up and said,
"I see people; they look like trees walking around."

MARK 8:23-24

There is nothing like a good shock to get us to wake up from our slumber and smell the coffee. A jolt to make us deal with the reality of where we are. Most of the time, situations aren't what they appear to be. We tend to make molehills into mountains. Our circumstances seem greater and more daunting than they really are. We lose our perspective in the midst of our pain.

What can we do? We need a spiritual realignment. We need to focus on the important things and not get stuck in the meaning of the trivial, of the things that have no bearing on anything really. And then it happens. Something that puts everything into perspective. Something unexpected shocks us and rocks our world.

We wonder, *Why did God allow such a thing?* The answer? For the sake of a greater spiritual awakening!

What can't you seem to overcome? How does it affect your outlook on life and what you do? How can you change your perspective?

Dear heavenly Father, help me see things from Your vantage point. In Jesus' name. Amen.

One More Touch

Once more Jesus put his hands on the man's eyes.
Then his eyes were opened, his sight was restored,
and he saw everything clearly.

MARK 8:25

"How many times must I go through this?" I've asked this many times, and the answer comes back, "As many times as is necessary for you to get it right." God is so patient. He will keep touching us in the same place until we allow Him to complete what He has begun in us. He wants us to see Him and His purpose for us clearly.

Are you struggling, trying to see your way through your pain, your brokenness, your disappointment with the way life has gone? Did a relationship disappoint you? God is eager to work with you. To touch your eyes. To touch your heart. To put everything in the right perspective. The world is not ending. You probably won't die because of this situation. And the chances are you will love again. You will recover. You will make it. You will be restored. Rest under God's touch, and let Him do what He does best—give you sight. His truth will set you free, liberate your heart, and give you eagles' wings to fly above your situation until you see what God sees—that no issue is insurmountable or unsolveable. And certainly no scenario is greater than the ability of God.

What issues are out of perspective for you right now? What do you need clarity on? Ask God to help you see clearly.

Dear heavenly Father, restore me and help me see things as You do. In Jesus' name. Amen.

Embracing Change

Jesus sent him home, saying, "Don't go into the village."
MARK 8:26

When we understand that where we've been shapes our outlook and affects our hearts, we'll become more selective of the places we frequent. After Jesus healed the man who couldn't see, the man was cautioned not to return to where he was. He was to go home. He didn't live where he was when Jesus healed him! And we don't have to live where we are emotionally either. This is crucial to maintaining victory in our lives.

Going back to the same way of doing things only deepens our bondage. Like the smoker who quits and then returns to smoking, he now finds the habit has gotten stronger. Jesus tells a parable comparing a man to a house. A demon returns to the house after it was cleaned and, finding the door open, brings seven friends with him! Now the state of that man is much worse than before. Revisiting the same old issues in our lives further entrenches their hold on us. We need to secure our liberty by slamming the door, moving on, and not looking back. Let go of old haunts, habits, and friends if necessary to stay free. We don't need to nurse and rehearse the same incidences. And let's praise God for His restoring touch!

What do you need to walk away from? What does looking back do to your recovery process? What happens when you revisit an issue or get caught up in repetitive conversations?

Dear heavenly Father, help me walk away from trouble and begin again in You. In Jesus' name. Amen.

Embracing the Truth

Jesus left the vicinity of Tyre and went through Sidon, down to the
Sea of Galilee and into the region of the Decapolis. There some
people brought to him a man who was deaf and could hardly talk,
and they begged him to place his hand on the man.

MARK 7:31-32

So many attend church every Sunday and sit in pews where the Word
of God is being declared. But then they walk away and live their lives
as if they never heard a word. And often what comes out of their mouths
and what they say they believe are contrary to God's Word. And then when
circumstances take a turn for the worse, these people blame God.

What you receive has everything to do with your mindset and your confession. What are you listening to? How well do you hear what God and
others are saying to you? And what about your friends? Do they accept your
biblically based counsel? If not, the only thing you can do is release them
to God. Continue to watch and pray but don't get dragged into their problems. Leave their problems...and them...at the feet of Jesus.

What truths are you running away from? Have people reached out with
the truth? How did you respond?

———————————— ❖ ————————————

*Dear heavenly Father, open my ears to hear and my heart to
change so I can better serve and honor You. In Jesus' name.
Amen.*

Hearing a Different Drummer

After he took him aside, away from the crowd,
Jesus put his fingers into the man's ears.
MARK 7:33

*J*esus calls us aside from all the other voices that try to drown Him out. By His Spirit, He silences the sounds that confuse and distract us from the truth. Be still and know that He alone is God. Our circumstances and what we see before us is not all there is. In the silence we'll hear His gentle whisper saying, "This is the way; walk in it" (Isaiah 30:21). Perhaps this was why Jesus broke away from the crowds to find solace with His Father.

The world can be a noisy place, screaming contrary messages that contest our faith and fill us with fear and uncertainty. In the midst of all the noise God invites us to steal away. We need to listen to Him, allow Him to place His hands over our ears, and move near to Him so we hear His heart. This gives us the strength to walk against the opposing winds of the world and follow the Holy Spirit. We walk to the beat of a different drummer... to the beating of our loving heavenly Father's heart.

What in your life drowns out the whisper of God's Spirit? What can you do to hear God more clearly?

———————————— ✺ ————————————

Dear heavenly Father, I need to hear You. Draw me close to You and open my ears. In Jesus' name. Amen.

Open to Options

Then [Jesus] spit and touched the man's tongue.
He looked up to heaven and with a deep sigh said to him,
"Ephphatha!" (which means, "Be opened!").

MARK 7:33-34

Sometimes God has to shock us to get us to be open to the other options available. So many people get so fixed on what they want that they fail to consider alternative ways to move forward. Our insistence on our way may hinder our ability to be in the best position to receive some of God's many blessings. If we insist our potential mates look certain ways, have particular professions, or be experienced in certain areas, we are limiting our options. If we insist on having specific things at certain times or in certain ways, we may get locked in patterns of disappointments, resulting in frustration. Expectations can be robbers of what we truly desire because we're limiting what we expect from God. He may be seeing many options available for our joy! So let's work on being more open to Him blessing us in different ways. He will! He is faithful and will give to us abundantly—beyond anything we could hope for or pray for.

What new options do you find when you open your heart and mind to God?

Dear heavenly Father, I choose to stop insisting on my own way. I open my hands, heart, and mind to You. Have Your way in my life. In Jesus' name. Amen.

The Gift of Revelation

At this, the man's ears were opened, his tongue
was loosened and he began to speak plainly.
MARK 7:35

*W*ith clear revelation comes the freedom to declare by faith what God has promised. Our words have the power to reinforce our beliefs and help us stay on course. This is why it's so important to discern what is true and what is false. If we constantly repeat errors, we may come to believe them or get discouraged by them. God's Word says to think on what is true, noble, right, pure, lovely, admirable, and praiseworthy (Philippians 4:8).

So let's be careful about what we say...speaking only when we hear the prompting of God clearly. Jesus repeated what He heard His Father say, and every word He spoke was filled with power and life. We can declare what God's Word says, knowing it's true and unadulterated. Stop, listen, absorb, and then repeat. What an amazing difference this can make in our lives!

What has stopped you from speaking the truth in the past? What truths do you need to revisit to adjust your attitude and mindset?

Dear heavenly Father, I know I've listened to the wrong things before, even repeated them and allowed them to contaminate my beliefs and what I have confessed in You. Forgive me. Grant me clarity so I will speak and stand only on the truth found in You and in what You have proclaimed. In Jesus' name. Amen.

Purity seems to be a foreign concept to our society. God holds His followers to a higher standard of living. He doesn't do this because He's prudish, uptight, or a killjoy. He does it to protect us and keep us free from the bondage and pain of misplaced affections. Anyone who has given themselves and then been rejected knows firsthand the desperate loneliness that follows. Our God is protective as a truly good father should be. He warns us to avoid the pain by guarding our hearts and setting boundaries that keep us safe from rejection and heartbreak. As we come into the full knowledge of what true love costs and the value of our hearts and our bodies, we'll make different choices that set us apart and help us embrace the liberty Christ has for us.

True Worship

I urge you, brothers, in view of God's mercy, to offer
your bodies as living sacrifices, holy and pleasing to God—
this is your spiritual act of worship.

ROMANS 12:1

The only problem with a living sacrifice is it keeps crawling off the altar. All joking aside, the apostle Paul puts sexual intimacy in perspective by asking us to consider the goodness of God toward us—His great and tender mercy, His willingness to rescue us, to pay the IOU for our sins, and to enable us to have close fellowship with Him again. In light of this, Paul is saying that it's a small sacrifice to give our bodies to the Lord as an act of worship. Walking in purity is a way of saying thank-you to God for all He's done for us. This is a major part of true worship—walking in obedience before God. Jesus said it best, "If you love me, you will obey what I command" (John 14:15).

Have you struggled to maintain purity before God? What will make it easier for you? What needs to change?

Dear heavenly Father, I long to please You in every way. Once again I surrender all that I am to You. In Jesus' name. Amen.

A Different Frame of Mind

Do not conform any longer to the pattern of this world,
but be transformed by the renewing of your mind. Then you
will be able to test and approve what God's will is—
his good, pleasing and perfect will.

ROMANS 12:2

As we are visually and audibly assaulted by the media with suggestive and often overt images of out-of-control sexuality, it becomes more and more difficult to keep our spiritual equilibrium. Purity is also much more than just a sexual issue. We need to strive to keep our speech pure, our thoughts pure, and our devotion pure. At times we ask, "Am I the only one trying to live holy?" Talk about being a salmon swimming upstream! But remember, the rest of the fish are being carried downstream by the current.

As believers in Christ, we are not of this world even though we're in it. We are held to a higher standard of living by our Father God as examples to the world of what kingdom living looks like. There is no permissiveness with God. He wants us to abide by His good and perfect will. When we compromise, we send mixed signals to an already confused world of what God looks like and who His people really are, not to mention the cost to us spiritually, mentally, and physically. Though we aren't perfect, we need to set our minds to live God's way and do our best to follow through.

Are you struggling with purity? What are you clinging to by following your own will? What can you do to make following God's will easier in this area?

Dear heavenly Father, help me settle the raging battle inside of me. As my love for You increases, help me love what You love and hate what You hate. In Jesus' name. Amen.

Sound Judgment

"Everything is permissible for me"—but not everything
is beneficial. "Everything is permissible for me"—
but I will not be mastered by anything.

1 Corinthians 6:12

We can do all things through Christ who strengthens us (Philippians 4:13). This means we are empowered by Him to make the right choices. We can exercise the kind of discernment that sees there is no profit in sin, in partaking of things that weaken our spirits. There is loss when we grieve the Spirit of God. God has called us into the marvelous light of liberty in Him. We can choose freedom over bondage to the demands of our flesh and carnal minds.

As beings created to experience a full set of emotions and senses, our desires were approved by God—before the fall and sin entered the picture. Today we need to guard our purity and make sure our desires don't control us. This is a choice we get to make. We can use the leverage of our love for God to catapult us out of the stronghold of sin and the unholy actions that try to bind us and impede our walk with Him.

Paul said that when he was a child he thought as a child. A child has no discipline. But he also said that when he got older he put away childish things. One sign of spiritual maturity is exercising sound judgment—to separate what is a waste of time from what is an investment in kingdom living and personal victory.

What thoughts and actions tug at you most? Which are beneficial? Which threaten to master you? What can you do to be free?

———————————— ✺ ————————————

Dear heavenly Father, I know You know my struggles. Give me Your wisdom and help me make good judgments and triumph over sin through Your Son. In His name I pray. Amen.

Back to Basics

The body is not meant for sexual immorality,
but for the Lord, and the Lord for the body.
1 Corinthians 6:13

*L*et's put things in perspective. When we use things improperly there are always consequences. This is why we must understand God's design for us. When God first created man, sexuality was way down on the initial list of functions. There wasn't even a woman created yet! God gave the man a list of things to do with his body that had nothing to do with romance and intimacy. Adam was to take care of God's creation. His job was to work the ground and supervise all that God made. At the end of each day he met with God for a delightful exchange as he walked and talked with His Creator. Ah, divine fellowship. Doesn't it sound heavenly?

Sexual intimacy came long after that. It sealed the union of the covenant that was made between Adam and Eve. Under God's watchful eye, the marriage bed was blessed and undefiled as they experienced intimate communion.

Whether prostrating our bodies before the throne of grace in worship, using them to serve others, or giving them as gifts to our mates (after we're married, of course!), we dedicate who we are to the Lord. And as we walk before God with our bodies surrendered to Him, we'll find pleasure in all the dimensions our bodies were created to be used for.

In what ways have you taken your body back from God? What can you do to give it back and remain surrendered to Him?

———————————— ✠ ————————————

Dear heavenly Father, please forgive me for taking ownership of my body. I give it back to You now. In Jesus' name. Amen.

Intimate Oneness

Do you not know that he who unites himself with a prostitute is one
with her in body? For it is said, "The two will become one flesh."
But he who unites himself with the Lord is one with him in spirit.

1 CORINTHIANS 6:16-17

When we understand the profound depth of what sex truly is, perhaps then we'll respect the power of passion. In biblical times, men went to pagan temples to sleep with prostitutes as part of their worship. This is the religious society Paul is speaking about when he warns against taking sex casually. The spiritual implication of binding soul to soul as well as body to body is serious and far-reaching. It's not to be taken lightly. The word "know" is used in reference to sexual intimacy in many Scripture verses, such as "Now Adam knew Eve his wife, and she conceived and bore Cain" (Genesis 4:1 NKJV).

In a similar but nonsexual way, when we "know" God, we become one with Him and conceive of the fruit of the Spirit, who gives us the power to bear the attributes of Christ to the world. But when we join with others outside of God's design for intimacy, our worship becomes perverted. We have become one with people who aren't intent on honoring God or us. Small wonder that people who approach sex lightly usually experience heartache. Sex is binding. In essence, you're giving part of you to the other person, and you can't get it back. Be careful lest you become ensnared.

Has honoring God by exercising control in purity been difficult for you? What steps can you take to guard your heart and spirit and body?

Dear heavenly Father, I want to be joined to You and follow Your standards. Help me honor You with my body. Give me the strength to remain pure sexually as I wait for the person You've chosen as my mate. As long as I'm single, help me handle my desires so I can remain pure for You. In Jesus' name. Amen.

The Deterioration of Sin

Flee from sexual immorality. All other sins a man [or woman]
commits are outside his body, but he who sins sexually
sins against his own body.

1 CORINTHIANS 6:18

We have only to look at the litany of sexually transmitted diseases to know the harm that intimate encounters can cause. But beyond the physical aspects, our spirits are also affected. For every encounter that makes us one with another, we give a portion of ourselves away. A connection is made that can't be severed.

Long after our "temporary partners" have departed, we'll feel empty and uneasy, knowing we've violated God's standards. The pain of rejection and regret will persist. Shame exacerbates the issue, and the damage done to our hearts and souls can be long lasting. Yes, there are sins outside the body we can walk away from. The consequences are one-hit wonders that we may gloss over. But when we sin against our bodies, we mar God's design for our wholeness. Our only permanent relief and restoration comes from God as we go to Him and confess our sins, ask for forgiveness, and request His strength to stay on His path in the future. Although we may not get the "piece" of us back that we gave away, we do get *God's peace* that completely fills in what we lost.

Only within the safe confines of marriage can we gain something permanent and truly intimate from sexual encounters. As we give ourselves to our God-given husbands, we are richer for the exchange.

Have you sinned with your body? What were the consequences? What did you learn? What will you do differently now?

———————————— ✠ ————————————

*Dear heavenly Father, when I misuse the body and senses
You gave me, I sin against You. Forgive me and keep me safe
and pure in You. In Jesus' name. Amen.*

We Are Temples

Do you not know that your body is a temple of the Holy Spirit,
who is in you, whom you have received from God?
You are not your own.

1 CORINTHIANS 6:19

One of the great justifications for sexuality and related subjects is, "It's my body. I can do what I want with it!" This cry is used to excuse or permit sexual promiscuity, abortion, drug abuse, and much more. But your body is not your own. It belongs to the One who created it!

When we accept Christ, the Holy Spirit takes up residence within us. The Spirit of God is present wherever we go, whatever we do. He is privy to every conversation we have. He hears every whisper. He sees what we do in the dark and in the light. Our bodies are temples where He abides.

How often have we taken Him into situations He doesn't approve of or want to participate in? I once heard a preacher ask a congregation, "What is rape?" The people responded by saying it's an act of someone being taken against his or her will. The pastor responded that a lot of people subject the Holy Spirit to rape by submitting Him to acts He wants no part of. A hush fell over the congregation. It was a harsh picture, but everyone got the full impact of his statement. Perhaps if we were more willing to acknowledge the presence of God at all times, our conduct and conversation would change.

What will it take to make you more cognizant of God's presence in your life? What areas of conversation and conduct need to change in your life in light of His presence?

Dear heavenly Father forgive me for the times I've subjected You to things You didn't want to be part of. Help me be more aware of Your constant presence, strength, and love. In Jesus' name. Amen.

The Value of Your Body

You were bought at a price. Therefore honor God with your body.

1 CORINTHIANS 6:20

*H*ow would you feel if you gave someone an expensive gift and every time you saw them, the item you'd given looked worse because it wasn't properly cared for? What an insult to you. What an ungrateful heart the recipient is showing. Few things offend more deeply than lack of appreciation. We want to say, "Don't you know how much I paid for that? Don't you know what the gift represents—my love for you?"

Perhaps these are God's sentiments exactly. Remember how much He paid for us? The costly sacrifice of His beloved Son is reason enough for us to treat our bodies as extremely valuable. This honors God. We need to care for our bodies. We need to protect them by supplying the proper diet, exercise, rest, and so forth.

So, prize your body, protect it, treat it well to the glory of God.

In what ways have you taken your body for granted or abused it? What can you do to honor God with your body? What are the benefits for you?

———————————— ✠ ————————————

Dear heavenly Father, please forgive me for taking my body for granted and not recognizing its value. Show me the best way to honor You with my body. In Jesus' name. Amen.

Representing Christ

It is God's will that you should be sanctified: that you should avoid sexual immorality; that each of you should learn to control [her] own body in a way that is holy and honorable, not in passionate lust like the heathen, who do not know God.

1 Thessalonians 4:3-4

*W*hat will separate us from the masses? Our knowledge of God. Our healthy fear of the Lord that translates to wisdom. The discipline of self-control. The discernment to embrace and implement the knowledge we have from Scripture that calls us to a life set apart to God.

Controlling our bodies in areas that range from food to sex is something that is learned. Many people have said, "If God wants me to abstain from sex until I'm married, why doesn't He take the feelings and desires away until then?" God isn't going to do that. He gave us a beautiful gift called "free will," and He wants us to exercise that free will wisely. He wants us to grow strong in self-discipline and control. He wants us to come to Him when we need help.

Passion needs to be reserved for the purposes of God and the marriage bed. In all aspects of life we are to walk circumspectly, redeeming our time by living sanctified lives. This is how God's standards are revealed so the people around us can be enticed to God through His peace and love exhibited through our actions. This testimony speaks more loudly than words ever can.

How has your walk with the Lord affected those around you? How apparent is it that your life is different from those who don't know God? How does your life inspire others to want to know the Lord?

Dear heavenly Father, I am humbled by the investment You've made in me. Teach me how to live surrendered to You from the inside out. In Jesus' name. Amen.

The Power of Influence

In this matter [sexual immorality] no one should wrong his brother
or take advantage of him. The Lord will punish [people] for all such
sins, as we have already told you and warned you. For God
did not call us to be impure, but to live a holy life.

1 Thessalonians 4:6-7

*M*any women have chafed and been resentful that most of the time it seems they are the ones who have to set the standard for holiness in romantic relationships. Why aren't men held accountable too? Perhaps it's time to take another look at why *both* need to keep each other honorable before God. Our heavenly Father holds us accountable for how we treat others, including whether we take advantage of another person's vulnerabilities. We are to provoke one another to *good* works and *right* living before God.

Eve did not escape judgment in the garden for disobeying God and influencing Adam to do the same. Adam was judged for listening to her and sinning against God's command. God wants us to be whole and healthy. This is why He insists on a walk of holiness for men and women.

Have you thought about how much influence you have with others? You might be surprised! Why is it important to set personal boundaries? How does your restraint or lack of restraint affect others?

Dear heavenly Father, help me to always be an influence for holiness. In Jesus' name. Amen.

Consider the Source

He who rejects this instruction [on purity] does not
reject man but God, who gives you his Holy Spirit.

1 Thessalonians 4:8

My mother always said that opinions are like noses. Everyone has one. When all our conversations and debating are done, there is only one opinion that really matters—God's. He had the first say, and He will have the last. While many Bible studies emphasize how the teachings affect you and what they mean to you, an important question to ask is, What does this mean to God? As we come to know and understand the heart of God by spending time in His Word and in prayer, we internalize more and more of His character. As we submit to His Word, maturity in Christ buds and our minds and hearts are transformed to be more like Christ's.

Our human knee-jerk reaction to correction should diminish as we experience the loving discipline and instruction from our holy, compassionate, and understanding God. And when people correct us, let's look for God's truth in their words and respond to that instead of reacting to the person or to the idea of being confronted.

We don't need to fear people. They have no power over our eternal destiny. The argument about the mandates that lead to holiness is not with man, it is with God, and in light of who He is and what He knows, there can be no argument at all.

In what ways do you struggle with God's instruction? Why do you take things personally? How can allowing yourself to be corrected and instructed benefit you?

Dear heavenly Father, forgive me for the times I rebel against Your instruction. Help me fall in love with You and Your Word so I will surrender willingly. In Jesus' name. Amen.

Understanding who we are in Christ and what we're called to brings us peace as we grow. Life is seasonal, and change is inevitable. So *carpe diem*! Seize the day! Life is too short to spend chasing tomorrow. Take one day at a time and live fully in the moment.

The present is a gift. As we surrender to where God has us right now, we will spot more roses than thorns in our journey through life's garden. In all growth there is a period of dormancy, when plants gather energy and build up strength. The same is true for us. This doesn't take away from our expectancy for the desire of our hearts. It merely puts life in perspective and gives us the power to wait patiently, knowing God will be victorious and will have us bear fruit. And our fruit will get sweeter with time and furnish a bounty to God, to others, and to ourselves. So live in the moment. Seek God for what He wants you to do right now. Tomorrow and all that it brings will come soon enough.

Dwelling in the Present

Each one should retain the place in life that the Lord
assigned to him and to which God has called him.
1 CORINTHIANS 7:17

*I*f you're following God, studying His Word, and living for Jesus,
where you are in life right now is your present assignment. Do the
work that is required.

Often when we face assignments or tasks we don't like, we don't invest
ourselves 100 percent. In essence we are "done," even though we might not
be finished with the project. We need to finish each phase and season of our
lives. This will be a delight as we grow and mature in Christ.

In hindsight there are always things about the previous life season we
wish we'd appreciated more. As the adage says, "We never miss the water till
the well runs dry." We have the awesome privilege of being free to pursue
all that is in our hearts right now. But we won't reap the rewards and satisfaction if we are so focused on tomorrow that we're not paying attention to
today. Let's rejoice in where we are.

Do you dwell more in the past, present, or future? If you've missed something by overlooking the present, what were the consequences? What can
you do to embrace the present more joyfully?

---

*Dear heavenly Father, help me grow joyously where You've
planted me. In Jesus' name. Amen.*

Embrace the Liberty

*I would like you to be free from concern. An unmarried man
is concerned about the Lord's affairs—how he can please
the Lord. But a married man is concerned about the affairs of this
world—how he can please his wife—and his interests are divided.*

1 Corinthians 7:32-34

When I first read this Scripture passage, I wondered what singles Paul had met and what he was emphasizing. Was he encouraging singles to spend more time thinking of how to serve God? Perhaps if I were rewriting Paul's letter today I would simply say that everything has a price.

If we're looking longingly at the prospects of marriage, we may be viewing that state through rose-colored lenses. Many a married person wishes to be single. So while we think the grass looks greener on the other side, let's remember that the people on the far side of the fence work hard to make their marriages click. That takes a lot of energy!

Far too often we take for granted the freedom afforded us as single women. In some aspects life is difficult because the weight of maintaining a household, paying for groceries, bringing in an income, and so forth falls directly on us. But the flip side is we only have to deal with the lessons we're learning. We are free to serve God, as well as live life to the fullest, without the obligation to make sure a partner is doing okay, is growing, and has what he or she needs. As singles we can usually choose what work and activities and causes we want to be involved in. And that my friend should give us great joy! Let's not take our present freedom for granted. Tomorrow things could change.

What liberties can you celebrate as a single right now? What would change in your life if you got married right now? What would you miss the most?

---- ❖ ----

*Dear heavenly Father, forgive me for taking the freedom I've
been given for granted. Help me turn my sights to pleasing You
and appreciating where You have me right now. Amen.*

A Surrendered Heart

*An unmarried woman or virgin is concerned about
the Lord's affairs: Her aim is to be devoted to the Lord
in both body and spirit. But a married woman is concerned about
the affairs of this world—how she can please her husband.*

1 Corinthians 7:34

C an we talk about devoting our attention, affection, minds, bodies, and spirits to the Lord? "Single-hearted devotion," I call it. At one point when I was struggling with my joy level and waiting on God for my knight in shining armor, one of my ex-boyfriends said, "You know, Michelle, waiting on God doesn't mean you sit in His lap and keep looking over His shoulder to see if what you want is coming. It means you sit in His lap and give Him your full attention." This made me angry at the time because I was guilty of doing exactly what he'd said. I was looking past God to the empty horizon and getting more frustrated by the minute. My heart was divided between God and my desire for a husband.

I finally got to the place where I was able to take my eyes off my biological clock and what I wanted. I focused on God and His will for my life completely. And I discovered a joy I didn't know existed! As I got caught up in Him, I found purpose and fulfillment beyond my imagination. A surrendered heart free of distraction is the key to being a joyful single woman. As we're caught up in the love of the Lord, we are finally free to celebrate the life we've been given and know God will provide for us in due time.

Where is your focus today? What is most important to you right now? How can you find fulfillment where you are right now?

———————————— ✠ ————————————

*Dear heavenly Father, teach me how to love You more. I want to
set my affections completely on You. In Jesus' name. Amen.*

Getting Rid of the Weight

Let us throw off everything that hinders and the sin
that so easily entangles, and let us run with
perseverance the race marked out for us.

HEBREWS 12:1

When I walk my dogs I'm careful to go unencumbered. This prevents me from getting tired, distracted, and weighed down so I can enjoy the walk. If I have to carry packages, I've found that I'm not willing to go very far. I turn back after a short time, too tired to continue. Life is like that too. Too often we drag junk around. And I'm not just talking about obvious sins or transgressions. We make life more exhausting than it needs to be and wear ourselves out unnecessarily. Why? Our mindsets, unhealthy habits, unprofitable distractions, and unfruitful relationships sap our energy. So let's get rid of them! They only hinder our progress and make us too short-winded to persevere.

God has determined a route for our lives. But many things can stand in the way of us clearly seeing the path and enjoying the journey. What can we do? Evaluate our lives and look for distractions, lingering problems, and places where we're spinning our wheels. God wants us to walk and not grow weary, to run and win life's race with flying colors. We've got places to go and things to do for God, sister!

What has been slowing down your progress spiritually? Physically? Emotionally? Professionally?

———————————————— ✠ ————————————————

Dear heavenly Father, show me the distractions and weights that keep me from becoming all You created me to be. Then help me eliminate them. In Jesus' name. Amen.

The Necessity of Diligence

If you think you are standing firm, be careful that you don't fall!

1 CORINTHIANS 10:12

The most dangerous thing a soldier can do is relax. He must remain on guard and alert. Our Lord understood the importance of persistent diligence. Jesus withstood being tempted by the devil in the wilderness (Matthew 4:1-11). And so it is with us. Satan is looking for people who have their guards down. Those who have become so secure in their belief they are invincible that they've relaxed their watch against the things that tempt and provoke. This is when mistakes are made and the strongest of saints can falter and fall. The tempter also looks for people so caught up in their problems or world that they've lost sight of their primary focus—God—so they are vulnerable to being led astray.

What can we learn from this? We should never think we are beyond temptation or past the possibility of falling into sin. Every athlete or performer knows relaxing is the enemy of excellence. A bit of tension is good. It keeps us sharp. It keeps us victorious.

In what areas are you relaxing? When you relax, what types of things fall through the cracks? What changes do you need to make to your approach in these areas?

Dear heavenly Father, help me remain diligent. I want to always be effective in my witness of You. Help me be productive and pleasing to You. In Jesus' name. Amen.

The Power to Resist

No temptation has seized you except what is common to man.
And God is faithful; he will not let you be tempted beyond
what you can bear. But when you are tempted, he will also
provide a way out so that you can stand up under it.

1 CORINTHIANS 10:13

I've been asked many times why God doesn't just take our desires away or prevent circumstances that may cause us to falter in our faith or our determination to follow Him. The answer is simple. He wants us to be the master of our desires. This is where we get to shine as saints of God. We're setting an example for the world. Where is victory if there hasn't been resistance? When we overcome the temptations of life, our witness is strengthened, God is glorified, and many are influenced for the kingdom.

God has promised to give us the tools we need to escape temptation. He also promises to restore us when we fail and then return to Him. As my mother used to say when I would lament not being able to do something, "You're really not missing anything." I've discovered that I did miss something—the consequences of falling prey to temptation!

We are not alone during this life on earth. We have a loving heavenly Father, the Holy Spirit, and Jesus! They will help us stand strong against temptation. The choice is ours. God cheers us on. He believes in us. He knows we can make the right choices and grow in Him. And when temptation comes, God will be faithful to make a way of escape...our job is to take it!

What temptations are you most prone to? In what ways do you wrestle with this? What do you need to do to allow God to help you?

———————————— ⸙ ————————————

Dear heavenly Father, deliver me from temptation. In Jesus' name. Amen.

Don't Turn Back

It is for freedom that Christ has set us free. Stand firm, then,
and do not let yourselves be burdened again by a yoke of slavery.
GALATIANS 5:1

*D*on't go back the way you came. That's what today's verse is telling us. In many instances we romanticize the past. Relationships and situations that were not good for us look a lot rosier once some time has passed by. Like the Israelites who had fond memories of leeks and onions in Egypt, quickly forgetting the hard labor they endured while being forced to make bricks without straw, we sometimes regret our newfound freedom. How quickly the uncertainty of the future makes us forget past pain! God's design for our lives doesn't include unnecessary hardship and unfruitful exchanges. The steps He has ordered for us lead to a place of righteousness, peace, joy, and completion. He brings us liberty!

Jesus came that we might have abundant life—not the angst of relationships and circumstances that place us in bondage and drain our lifeblood. So no matter how lonely we feel, let's don't go back to the situations that will multiply our pain. We can stand firm knowing this too will pass. The life and love we truly want is waiting for us and will come in God's perfect timing.

What situation or relationship from your past are you romanticizing? What advantages would you realize if you went back? What would be the drawbacks?

Dear heavenly Father, help me trust You in times of uncertainty. Give me patience as I wait for Your deliverance and embrace the freedom You give. In Jesus' name. Amen.

Love Begins with You

You...were called to be free. But do not use your freedom
to indulge the sinful nature; rather, serve one another in love.
The entire law is summed up in a single command:
"Love your neighbor as yourself."
GALATIANS 5:13-14

God knows our hearts" is a popular phrase and is often used next to references to His grace. But grace was never meant to give us a covering as we deliberately sin by assuring us God will forgive us. If we truly purpose to live true to the Word of God, the basic premise is simple. When we follow the first two commandments treating people with respect and love, as the Bible teaches, becomes doable. If we truly love God, our neighbors, and ourselves, we won't be selfish, insensitive, impatient, or even easily offended. We will be giving, understanding, and caring. We will bear each other's burdens and step in to help when the weaknesses of others are revealed. And we won't insist on credit because that is what love does. It seeks to bring out the best in others and forgives much, giving us and others grace in our humanity.

What does this mean for us? That we must begin with ourselves. Perhaps God is as forgiving as He is because He is secure in who He is. He knows He is God even when we don't respond positively to Him. He remains the great I Am. As we rejoice in who we are and embrace our identity in Christ, we are free to celebrate and love others without fear of hurt or disappointment. And that allows us to experience and release God's grace on a new level.

In what ways do you struggle to love others? What affects your self-esteem? How is your response to others related to how you feel about yourself?

———————————— ⁘ ————————————

Dear heavenly Father, show me who I am in You. Help me love myself as You love me so I can freely love others and tell them about You. In Jesus' name. Amen.

The Right Focus

I pray that out of his glorious riches he may strengthen
you with power through his Spirit in your inner being,
so that Christ may dwell in your hearts through faith.

EPHESIANS 3:16-17

*I*n the realm of physical exercise, the latest rage is "core training."
The belief is that if our core, or midsection, is strong, the rest of
our body will be supported properly. That will result in being stronger and
healthier overall. The same can be said of faith. Our core beliefs drive our
thoughts, attitudes, and actions, which affect our lives. Our inner lives
affect our outer lives.

Where is our faith? Perhaps we need to evaluate what we believe to
make sure we're still on target. Christ is the center of our faith. We believe,
based on God's Word, that He is the rewarder of all who diligently seek
him. Our faith isn't in people. It's in Christ alone, who always loves us and
always delivers on His promises.

As we walk in obedience, we please God. And then He leads us to the
desires of our hearts because He can trust us with them. The power to walk
in the confidence that Christ is who He says He is, is an amazing gift!

Are there parts of God's Word you struggle to believe? What makes it so
difficult? What is at the core of your unbelief? What do you need to do?

---

*Dear heavenly Father, I've spent far too much time focusing
on my circumstances instead of looking to You for strength
and understanding. Grant me the power to stand in faith in
You. In Jesus' name. Amen.*

The Love of God

I pray that you, being rooted and established in love,
may have power, together with all the saints, to grasp how wide
and long and high and deep is the love of Christ, and to know
this love that surpasses knowledge—that you may be
filled to the measure of all the fullness of God.

EPHESIANS 3:17-19

If you're like me, you've heard many times that "the hole in your heart is not a person-sized hole. It's a God-sized hole." But circumstances happen that can make us forget that. Then we try to fill the vacuum with relationships (especially romantic ones), possessions, achievements, and other things we strive for on our own. As time goes by, despair and unhappiness bring us back to the cross of Jesus and what He did to set us free.

How can we truly comprehend a love that surpasses knowledge? In our limited human estimation of love it's difficult to grasp the depth and determination of God's love for us. How can anyone—even God—continue loving us when we are completely unlovable and go off on our own? We will probably never understand until we see Him face-to-face...and maybe not even then! But He blesses us with His love anyway. Perhaps the greatest leap of faith is to accept that God loves us no matter what. He loves us unconditionally. He loves us in spite of ourselves. We need to let this knowledge fill our hearts to overflowing.

How have you searched for love? In what ways have you been left wanting? Have you accepted and experienced God's amazing love through His Son? If not, why not do it now? Invite Jesus to be your Lord and Savior.

Dear heavenly Father, grant me the knowledge of Your love for me. Help me to rest in it and share it with others. In Your Son's name. Amen.

Take the Limits Off

Now to him who is able to do immeasurably more than all we
ask or imagine, according to his power that is at work within us,
to him be glory in the church and in Christ Jesus throughout
all generations, for ever and ever! Amen.

EPHESIANS 3:20-21

*Y*es, it's true. Most of the time we think way too small. We become so focused on our idea of what would make life better that we limit ourselves and the scope of our possibilities. We are capable of so much more! More joy, more fulfillment, more awesome relationships and experiences—if we will only utilize half the love and gifts God has created in us. Do we really know all we have?

Most of us are like a driver who owns a Porsche but never drives it over 25 mph. What a waste of so much power! My mechanic recently told me my car's engine light was on because I didn't drive it enough. Carbon had built up that caused parts to get clogged because they weren't being blown out regularly enough. One drive at highway speed cleared up the problem. Some of us need to rev up our engines and allow the power of God to be loosed full throttle in our lives! Perhaps the longing and dissatisfaction we feel is the Spirit of God impatiently waiting for us to stretch out and allow Him full access. As we live life to the fullest in Him, we'll be astounded at what awaits us. Partner with God today and let Him have complete control!

What has been stopping you from living the life God has for you? How have you hindered His plans?

———————————— ⌖ ————————————

Dear heavenly Father, help me use all You've given me as I serve You and reach out to others in Your name. I want to live my life to the utmost in You. In Jesus' name. Amen.

God Thought
of Everything!

God has given us everything we need to live this thing called "the single life." There is no excuse for not living life to the fullest. When we come to know Christ, we are empowered to live abundantly—filled with joy, peace, rich relationships, amazing purpose, and unspeakable fulfillment. God is our ultimate reward. With Him comes all the love we've been seeking. We were created for love by the ultimate Love!

How can we live life to the fullest even in less than perfect circumstances? By using the tools God provides through His Word. As we follow the instructions God has lovingly laid out for us, we make an amazing discovery. He has thought of everything we need to survive and thrive...and He makes sure we get them!

A Life Worth Living

I urge you to live a life worthy of the calling you have received.
EPHESIANS 4:1

What does a "life worthy of the calling of Christ" look like? Righteous and holy. Sound character and excellence that glorifies God and blesses others. Many people in the public eye have spurned the idea that they are role models. Through the media we are privy to every foolish move and bad mistake they make. Unfortunately, many people lack discernment to understand that the ways of the world lead to unhappiness and promote spiritual death. So the influence of celebrities makes a huge impact on the mores of our society. From the clothes they wear to their sexual promiscuity, they affect almost every aspect of our culture.

Did you know Christians can have similar influence? The world will notice if we rise to the full stature of what we were created to be in Christ. He gives us the power to influence people for God. It is imperative we raise the bar and set a high standard so people will want to know our heavenly Father who loves them. Have you noticed the disappointment exhibited when a prominent person who has a relationship with Christ compromises his or her standards? It makes the headlines and all the talk shows.

Even though the attitude may come across as derisive, many people want to believe there is something worth taking a stand for. They want hope. In times of persecution Christianity flourishes. Even today under harsh government regimes Christianity grows as people cry out to God. We have the opportunity to reflect God in a way that causes the world to seek Him.

When people look at your life, what do they see? In what ways do you reflect God? Have you noticed any results?

———————————————— ❖ ————————————————

Dear heavenly Father, help me be a worthy reflection of You for Your glory. In Jesus' name. Amen.

The Gift of Grace

To each one of us grace has been given as Christ apportioned it.
Ephesians 4:7

God carefully disperses His grace according to our need. When we need it, He delivers. Grace goes beyond the power of salvation. It gives us the strength to obey God. In His graciousness, God doesn't ask or expect us to do something He hasn't equipped us to do. His grace is the keeping power we need when we come to the end of our own strength. By His grace we overcome the trials of this life.

God understands that our endurance is relative to who we are (human!) and how we've been conditioned to respond to circumstances in light of what we've learned and experienced. In the times when we feel we're being stretched to the limit, we can be confident that God is working in our lives and His grace is sufficient to get us through His refining process. Rest in God's grace. Embrace it. Use it to get through. We can be all God created us to be. By His grace He makes it possible!

How can you draw on God's grace in your everyday struggles? Have you ever used God's grace as an excuse? What can you do to be more proactive in living a life that pleases God?

———————————— ✠ ————————————

Dear heavenly Father, thank You for Your grace. When I'm weak, remind me how much You love me and cover me with Your grace and strength. In Jesus' name. Amen.

A New Life

You were taught, with regard to your former way of life…
to be made new in the attitude of your minds; and to put on the
new self, created to be like God in true righteousness and holiness.

EPHESIANS 4:22-23

*W*ant a new life? Get a new attitude. A new mindset. A new way of looking at the world. A new view of you and what you can contribute. But do this in light of the new life God has given you through His Son, Jesus Christ.

Walking in true righteousness and holiness is going to create change in our world because the stand we take and the decisions we make based on God's Word will impact every aspect of our lives. New life comes to us through God. As we allow Him to renew our minds on how to do life, do relationships, do our careers, we'll move forward in His plan. There will always be room for improvement and reinvention because we're limited by our humanity. God is in the miracle business! As we grow in Him, the outer pieces of our lives will fall into place.

In what areas does your mindset need to line up more with God's? In what ways have you battled with walking in holiness? What attitudes do you need to change to please God more?

Dear heavenly Father, show me the areas I need to take another look at in my life. Renew my mind so I'll be in agreement with You. In Jesus' name. Amen.

Decisions, Decisions

Be very careful, then, how you live—not as unwise but as wise,
making the most of every opportunity, because the days are evil.

EPHESIANS 5:15

As Christians it's not wise to spiritualize our way through life. We don't want to be guided by our feelings or inclinations. Some of us can be so heavenly minded we're no earthly good. The Bible says faith without works is dead, so we must engage the wisdom God so freely gives as we make choices in every situation we face. More than ever we must use our God-given discernment in who to trust—who we allow into our lives, our hearts, our homes, and our businesses. We must ask God to help us accomplish His purposes.

The Bible mentions silly or weak-willed women laden with sin and swayed by all kinds of evil desires being taken captive by unsavory men (2 Timothy 3:2-6). It's time to wise up. The devil sees what we like and plays on our vulnerabilities. We need to check everything through God's Word, seek God, and make informed decisions. The choices we make today affect our tomorrows and the tomorrows of those around us.

What not-so-great decisions have you made that you're still paying for today? What have you learned from them?

———————————————— ✠ ————————————————

Dear heavenly Father, grant me Your divine wisdom. Let Your counsel reign in my heart when I make choices. In Jesus' name. Amen.

Life in the Right Light

Do not be foolish, but understand what the Lord's will is.

EPHESIANS 5:17

The Lord's will for your life puts everything into the right perspective. A hitchhiker chooses who to ride with based on the direction the driver is going. If the car isn't going his way, he doesn't accept the ride. We need to make wise choices today about where we're going and who we're walking with based on our knowledge of what God has called us to do.

Are the people in our lives walking toward Christ? Are they walking in a way that supports and complements God's call on our lives? Do they add or subtract from our commitment to be all God has called us to be? These questions apply to our activities and other areas of involvement too. Everything in our lives should be moving us toward our God-ordained futures. Let's do away with distractions and weights that may be enjoyable for the moment but add nothing to the larger picture of our lives in Christ. People who excel in life are fiercely focused. They don't have time for foolishness. Neither do we.

What is God's will for your life? How do your present circumstances and associations support that? Do you need to let go of anything?

———————————————— ✠ ————————————————

Dear heavenly Father, help me judge my choices in light of Your wisdom and Your will for my life. In Jesus' name. Amen.

The Strength to Make It

Be strong in the Lord and in his mighty power.
EPHESIANS 6:10

Not by our personal might or power will anything be accomplished or sustained. Only through God's Spirit are we empowered to run this race of life consistently and do great things for God and mankind. As a single woman, I feel the weight of my entire world upon my shoulders at times. I have to do everything. There is no one else. If I don't do it, it doesn't get done.

As I'm prone to tell people, "It's just me and Jesus at my house. And though He gives the power to gain wealth and promotion comes from Him, I have to give Him something to work with." I understand that as my faithful counselor, He grants me divine direction and then gives me the strength to do what I must do. Still I sometimes find myself feeling depleted from time to time. In those moments I need to draw back and rest in Him. I wait and allow Him to refuel me. I am on empty. There is no more "I." Only Christ in me is left. And that is when I get more done!

What happens when you run on your own steam? How can you tap into God's strength to sustain and empower you? What attitudes and beliefs do you need to do away with to more fully embrace the Lord's strength?

Dear heavenly Father, in so many instances my pride in my own sufficiency gets me in trouble. Help me rest in Your strength and allow You to restore and sustain me. In Jesus' name. Amen.

Dressing for Success

Put on the full armor of God so that you can take
your stand against the devil's schemes.
EPHESIANS 6:11

God's got us covered, but we must be willing to wear the garments He supplies for our protection. At times the weight of them may seem to be too much to bear, but He will ground us and keep us safe. The reality we must accept is that we have an enemy. An active, vigilant enemy. Satan has spent time studying us. He knows our weaknesses and waits patiently to stage his attack. God has promised to make a way of escape from the devil's plots and plans, but we must choose to take it. This is part of our training as soldiers in the kingdom of God. There is a uniform that identifies who we are and whose army we belong to. When we are fully fitted, we can stand firm in our convictions. The uniform lets everyone know where we stand... and where we refuse to fall.

Are you missing any parts of your armor? Why not read Ephesians 6:11-18 to get the full picture of what God provides? Then you'll be fully suited to face life and resist temptation.

Dear heavenly Father, as I don the armor You provide, grant me the strength to stand firm for You. In Jesus' name. Amen.

Know the Enemy

For our struggle is not against flesh and blood, but against the
rulers, against the authorities, against the powers of this dark world
and against the spiritual forces of evil in the heavenly realms.

EPHESIANS 6:12

One of my favorite cartoons shows a character saying, "We've discovered the enemy, and the enemy is us." Sometimes we are our worst enemies. Sometimes we feel that others are the enemy. But we have an even greater enemy. One who is out to destroy our hope and faith in Christ. This enemy of our souls is usually invisible, but at times he does his work through the people around us who are vulnerable to his manipulation.

What can we do to protect ourselves? Depend on Christ and ask Him for discernment. Look beyond the person who has offended us or rejected us or done something worse to see who is behind the scenes. Satan is who we battle. Our principle fight is with him. He must be tackled in the Spirit of God, not by means of our weak flesh. Prayer, submitting to God, actively resisting the devil's attacks are the ways of war as we keep our souls, our minds, and our identities safe in Christ.

When something negative happens to us, let's take a moment to count to ten and pray for guidance. The true culprit will be revealed...and defeated through the power imparted to us by our omnipotent Father.

What is your initial reaction to things that hurt or offend you? How can you redirect your response?

---- ✠ ----

Dear heavenly Father, when the enemy attacks, help me respond by calling on Your spirit for wisdom and strength. In Jesus' name. Amen.

Taking a Stand

Put on the full armor of God, so that when the day of evil comes,
you may be able to stand your ground, and after you
have done everything, to stand.

EPHESIANS 6:13

The shepherd boy David refused to wear King Saul's armor when facing Goliath because he said it hadn't been proved in battle. He knew it would be fatal to fight in an outfit he wasn't used to wearing. Practice makes perfect and prepares us for the times when we need to utilize the tools God gives us to battle the devil. A good soldier never relaxes.

Today might be a good day. We might be in a season of peace. But life is cyclical. Eventually we'll face trials. In those times we can't afford to not be ready or we'll be knocked down. We want to stand tall and firm in Christ. How can we prepare to fight? By studying God's Word and using the weapons He provides. He will train us to use them. When we get exhausted and feel we can't go on, we stand strong and trust in the strength of our Lord. We're made stronger for battle by going through trials—loss, heartache, disappointment, even devastation. God is always with us. And He does what He does best—routs the enemy. Victory is ours in Jesus Christ. Amen!

What has shaken your faith in the past? What is your source of strength should this revisit you? How can you prepare for the battle that will surely come?

Dear heavenly Father, show me what to do when trials and temptation come. Grant me the discernment to know what to do as I stand firm in You. In Jesus' name. Amen.

Don't Believe the Hype

Stand firm then, with the belt of truth buckled around your waist,
with the breastplate of righteousness in place.
EPHESIANS 6:14

No matter what anyone says, we must stand on the truth or we will give in to hype. We live in an age where many peddle fear. The media incessantly gives us the dour financial, employment, and global forecasts that leave many bound in fear. In those moments, we need to rest in the comfort that covers our hearts—God's peace. We can don the breastplate of righteousness. The knowledge that we are in right standing with God guarantees His provision in times when many fear if they will have enough to survive. But we know Jehovah-jireh, our provider. We have favor with Him because of our relationship. He will make a way out of "no way" to supply all our needs according to His riches in glory by Christ Jesus. That is a truth we can take to the bank!

God will supply streams in the desert because He's said so in His Word. Those who don't know this truth cling to the false evidence that can appear so real. When the winds of negativity blow, adjust your belt. It will hold all the other pieces of your armor firmly in place.

What fears are you tempted to give in to if you don't remind yourself of God's promises?

--------------------------------- ✠ ---------------------------------

Dear heavenly Father, let Your truth resound in my mind and heart. Let Your truth ground me in the faith I need to stand tall in You. In Jesus' name. Amen.

Action-packed Faith

[Stand firm] with your feet fitted with the readiness
that comes from the gospel of peace. In addition to all this,
take up the shield of faith, with which you can extinguish
all the flaming arrows of the evil one.

EPHESIANS 6:15

When we're grounded in the Word, we're ready for anything. Our faith will take us to many interesting places. However, along the path we need to be aware of our adversary, the devil. Our trust in God is the only successful weapon against his devices. Our knowledge of God's faithfulness and what He has done for us will snuff out the power of the enemy's threats and suggestions. As we counter his negatives with Jesus and our faith in Him, Satan is silenced. What can he say in the face of God's track record?

After we've walked a while with God, our feet are trained to take on any terrain and stand secure. We will be accompanied by peace along the way because of our trust in God. And He's already earned our trust because He's shown Himself strong for us before.

We may be single, but we are not alone. We have a companion, a partner, a mate who sticks closer than a brother, who has our backs in every area of our lives. God is an ever-present source of help in time of need. Isn't that exciting!

What occurrences can you look back on and see how God came through for you? How did this build your faith? What lies from the enemy does Jesus silence in your life?

Dear heavenly Father, thank You for the peace You give in times of trouble. I pray my faith increases with each test. In Jesus' name. Amen.

The Source of True Power

Take the helmet of salvation and the sword of the Spirit,
which is the word of God.

EPHESIANS 6:17

The enemy of our souls knows that if he can mess up our minds he has an open gate to negatively impact our lives. Our helmets of salvation, part of our armor God provides, is essential. The knowledge of who we are and whose we are must be intact and strong. That understanding along with the knowledge of Christ Jesus and God's Word are anchors that will keep us secure no matter what storms rage in our lives. Everything that matters and gives us strong footholds are in these four areas.

Wield God's Word like a weapon. It preserves us and keeps much at bay that will try to threaten our security. The knowledge that God reveals of His heart and what He has placed in us let's us know and recognize His power at work in our lives. We can rest in His promises and not give the enemy a listening ear.

In boxing, a good fighter knows how to protect his vulnerable parts with one hand while thrusting with the other. We too must learn to fight offensively and keep standing and punching no matter how fast and hard the blows come. When we have the right equipment in place, it doesn't matter *what is going on.* Victory is assured in Christ Jesus.

What assaults your mind that you need to discard? What promises do you have from God that refute what you're struggling with?

———————————— ✠ ————————————

Dear heavenly Father, as I meditate on Your Word, let it come alive in me and be my defense in times of struggle. In Jesus' name. Amen.

A Prayer Away

And pray in the Spirit on all occasions with all kinds of
prayers and requests. With this in mind, be alert
and always keep on praying for all the saints.
EPHESIANS 6:18

*P*rayer is not a one-sided monologue. It is a two-way conversation between you and God. The beauty of conversing with Him is that He is a master communicator. He loves to commune with us. As we open the lines of communication with Him, He visits us and touches our hearts, our minds, our spirits through His Word, through others, and through His presence.

There are all sorts of ways to pray. The moments of solace where we steal away to be with our God are one way. But so are times of walking in the park and listening to His whispers in the wind. Or sometimes in the midst of conversations with others we feel a nudge from His Spirit. If we seek Him, we will find Him everywhere, always ready to listen, to speak into our lives, to give us direction.

Let this continuous dialogue fine-tune our hearing and our understanding. We can be sensitive to opportunities to be in prayer and make it our first response to every situation. Constant prayer is a seamless segue into intercession. As we remember others in prayer, we'll see the fruit of our labors, which will give us even more to talk about with the Lover of our souls.

How is your prayer life? What interferes when it comes to the time you spend with God? In what ways can you increase your prayer life and enjoy God's presence more?

Dear heavenly Father, I open my heart to communing with You. Meet with me today. In Jesus' name. Amen.

God is more than a caring Creator. He is a doting Father who spoils His children. He anticipates all we need and gives it to us freely. He watches our progress, cheering us on and anticipating our exploits. And why wouldn't He? He has equipped us for our journey and stands as a present source of help should we need Him. As we encounter various trials and adventures, we need to be aware of His companionship and support. We are not alone. Not only are we being kept by His ever-present Spirit, but we are also being escorted by the Lover of our souls, the One who sticks closer than a brother, grants wisdom, gives comfort, and offers strength. Our Father in heaven will never leave us or forsake us. And in the times when we are too weary to go further, He will strengthen us...and even carry us.

Fully Equipped

His divine power has given us everything we need for life and godliness through our knowledge of him who called us by his own
glory and goodness.

2 PETER 1:3

The more we know God, the more we will understand about life, who we are, and where all the pieces of our sometimes compli-cated journeys fit. We will also be able to balance what God requires of us with what we hope for ourselves. He has given us a never-ending reserve of power that equips us to deal with the ins and outs of life. His goodness is the impetus for us to walk in a way that is pleasing to Him.

We have no valid reason for not being who we were created to be. God has given us everything we need to live up to His expectations and fulfill our desires that are based in Him. We just have to use what we've been given! This is not the time to spiritualize life so we are no "earthly" good. God is practical. As we learn of Him and His ways, we can reflect His character and His wisdom in our everyday living. This will ultimately lead to victory when we approach life from God's point of view. So let's take the limiters off! Whether we're single, divorced, or widowed, God will meet us where we live and supply all our needs according to His infinite riches through Christ Jesus.

What area of your life is in question right now? What do you need to know about God to sustain you at this time?

———————————— ✠ ————————————

Dear heavenly Father, fill me with the knowledge of You above all things. In Jesus' name. Amen.

Looking like God

Through these he has given us his very great and precious
promises, so that through them you may participate in
the divine nature and escape the corruption
in the world caused by evil desires.

2 PETER 1:4

God has given us 30,000 promises in His Word! He is the only Being who never lies and is always faithful to keep His promises. Because of this, we can be confident that our obedience to Him will be met with His faithfulness and love. As we wrestle with the many temptations that assault us, we are empowered by God to escape the things that pull on our hearts and flesh. We can redirect our desires because our heavenly Father is faithful. We, like Christ, can choose to emulate God, to reflect His nature and character in our decisions.

We can recognize temptation for what it is and also see ahead of time the ramifications for many of our actions. As we mature in Christ, we spend less time learning lessons the hard way. The knowledge of God's goodness satisfies us and dulls our hunger for things that are not served from His hand. As our desires change, so do our actions. We become more and more in line with our heavenly Father's nature. We reflect who He is for the world to see.

What desires do you presently battle with? What do you need to know about God to ward off temptation? What desire in you finds the temptation attractive? How can you redirect that desire?

Dear heavenly Father, deliver me from evil. Conform my heart to look more like Yours. I want to be a joyous participant of Your nature. In Jesus' name. Amen.

Faith Supplements

His divine power has given us everything we need...
For this very reason, make every effort to add to
your faith goodness; and to goodness, knowledge.

2 PETER 2:3,5

*F*aith doesn't stand alone. It's supplemented and energized by how we live our lives. Faith is active and reflects what we believe. The more faith we have, the more liberated we will be to do what God calls us to do. Good character is a natural response to God because we believe God's way is the best way.

The more we see the benefits of doing life God's way, the stronger we become in our conviction to be obedient to His Word. This is because we know beyond the shadow of a doubt the rewards of living our lives in Him. Only our lack of knowledge and fear cause us to take chances we know we shouldn't. For instance, if we truly believe God has a special someone for us, we won't settle for people who don't reflect God's teachings and love.

Our confidence in God has everything to do with our character. What we believe about God and how He has called us to live will shape our choices. Our knowledge and study of the Holy One and His Word will give us the understanding and strength to choose God's way.

What fears conflict with your faith and affect your choices? In what areas do you struggle with doing life God's way? How can you stand firm in your faith?

———————————— ✤ ————————————

Dear heavenly Father, grant me the knowledge I need to build my faith in You. Guide my choices in Your direction. In Jesus' name. Amen.

Transforming Knowledge

Make every effort to add to your faith goodness; and to goodness,
knowledge; and to knowledge, self-control; and to self-control,
perseverance; and to perseverance, godliness.
2 PETER 1:6

*W*hen we know better, we should do better. I love how the Message Bible interprets 2 Peter 1:5-8: "So don't lose a minute in building on what you've been given, complementing your basic faith with good character, spiritual understanding, alert discipline, passionate patience, reverent wonder, warm friendliness, and generous love, each dimension fitting into and developing the others."

True knowledge is spiritual understanding. This means we see beyond worldly wisdom to a deeper understanding of things. We are given clarity by tapping into God's point of view. This gives us the power we need to know how to walk in alert discipline, being watchful for the sake of our souls' well-being. This also gives us passionate patience to wait for what God has for us. We feel an urgency to hold on for the ultimate prize, but it's coupled with a fear of God that is really a sense of wonder about His power and a healthy respect for Him and His Word.

In the days of old, when the Bible was being transcribed, every time a scribe wrote the name of God, he threw away the pen because God's name was held in such high reverence. The more casual we are in our approach to God, the more our standards can slip into a laissez-faire attitude and our discipline to study the Word will fade. There is a reason patience is also called long-suffering! In light of our knowledge of God and what He has in store for us, waiting on Him is not suffering at all.

What causes your self-control and perseverance to waver? In what ways do you need to adjust your perspective of God? How will this affect your choices?

─────────────── ✥ ───────────────

Dear heavenly Father, increase my knowledge of who You are. Grant me understanding. Please transform my heart. In Jesus' name. Amen.

The Path to Love

Make every effort to add to your faith goodness; and to goodness,
knowledge...and to godliness, brotherly kindness;
and to brotherly kindness, love.

2 PETER 1:7

Our reverent wonder for God affects our heart attitude. Envy, jealousy, strife, pride, and entitlement shouldn't exist when we believe in an all-consuming God. Our hearts should melt with love because God is love. We can't strive to reflect God and not walk in love.

God understands us, and His grace helps us to love like He does. He is passionately patient with us. He doesn't harbor feelings of insecurity that drive Him to belittle us. In like manner, we also should seek to exhort and edify others. This can only be done as we draw from God's heart to fill the empty places in our own. As our hearts become filled with the confidence of His love for us and we find our self-esteem in Him, we are liberated to celebrate and build up others. This kindness invites and encourages the love we seek. God's love for us overflows, filling us completely with Him. Start where you are by loving God. Through Him, love those who are available to be loved right now. Watch your love meter shoot past full.

Have you been looking for love in the wrong places?

———————————— ✠ ————————————

Dear heavenly Father, fill me with Your love, and help me pass Your love on to others. In Jesus' name. Amen.

The Fruitful Life

Make every effort to add to your faith goodness; and to goodness,
knowledge; and to knowledge, self-control; and to self-control,
perseverance; and to perseverance, godliness; and to godliness,
brotherly kindness; and to brotherly kindness, love. For if you
possess these qualities in increasing measure, they
will keep you from being ineffective and unproductive
in your knowledge of our Lord Jesus Christ.

2 PETER 1:5-8

*I*f we continue to grow, developing the qualities in today's passage, we will be forces to be reckoned with! Not only will we walk in favor with God, we will walk in favor with everyone who loves Him or is open to Him. Our faith will be contagious! Our lives will be of significant influence, bearing much fruit. We'll remain steady in our faith and please God. Everyone longs to be significant. We can touch our world and leave an indelible impression on hearts by choosing to reflect God's love and grace in every encounter.

Living life to the fullest each and every day in this manner opens the door for true and lasting success and the love we've been longing for. And we never know who is watching so we can help others come to God. Most people want to be involved with something good. At the end of the day, it's how we've lived for God and shared Him that gives our hearts lasting satisfaction.

What would you like people to say about you? What contributions would you like to make to the world? In what ways can you be more fruitful?

Dear heavenly Father, I want to be effective for Your kingdom and produce fruit to Your praise and glory. Help me continue to grow and increase in ways that make me a blessing to You and the people I connect with. In Jesus' name. Amen.

The Great Reward

Not that I have already obtained all this, or have already
been made perfect, but I press on to take hold of
that for which Christ Jesus took hold of me.

PHILIPPIANS 3:12

Have you had the pleasure of being pursued by someone who loves you? Of course you have! Christ pursued you. From the halls of heaven, across the expanse of earth, to the depths of hell and back, Christ passionately pursued you with the desire of claiming you for His own. For His praise and glory. For intimate fellowship. For reconciliation with the Father. Jesus gave everything He was and had to claim you.

In light of this understanding, we pursue Him and the purpose for which He pursued us. He didn't chase us to give us to someone else. He pursued us to marry us! And we get to work with Him to accomplish His purposes for our lives on earth. This is deep fulfillment.

When we finally land on the "X marks the spot" through the Spirit and work toward God's purpose for our lives, all the pieces fall into place and we see God more clearly. Now we're making sound decisions because we seek to protect what God has placed in us. Our hearts beat with a passion we've never known. This is true life and love. God is our great reward, and when we seek Him, He gives of Himself fully. In that moment we discover what we were really seeking.

What is the one thing you hope to attain before you leave this earth? What do you think Christ pursued you for?

———————————— ✠ ————————————

*Dear heavenly Father, help me keep my eye on the prize—
You! Grant me the strength to pursue You with all my heart. In
Jesus' name. Amen.*

The Love of God

I pray that you, being rooted and established in love, may have
power, together with all the saints, to grasp how wide and long
and high and deep is the love of Christ, and to know this love
that surpasses knowledge—that you may be filled to
the measure of all the fullness of God.

EPHESIANS 3:17-20

The dreams we have of being loved are dwarfed by the reality of God's love for us. Remember, Christ gave everything to have us. He is the ultimate Bridegroom. We will never be able to fully comprehend His love for us. It is vaster and deeper than we can imagine. Greater than what we can contain. I'm rendered speechless when I attempt to compare it to anything I've known. As I consider God's grace and His endless patience toward me, I get a small glimpse of His passion. Oh, that my heart could beat with the fervor He has! Oh, that I could have a measure of the zeal He has for me!

When I think of His love and stretch my arms toward heaven to reach Him to worship and to bask in His presence, I am made full. Filled to overflowing measure with His goodness. I am caught up by His Spirit to a place where there is no wanting or evidence of lack. Oh, to remain in this place, where in this moment I am completely satisfied and filled with more love than I thought possible. That time will come! Can you relate?

What is lacking in your life? In your heart? Where do you find satisfaction and fulfillment? Is it enough?

———————————————— ❊ ————————————————

*Dear heavenly Father, as I rest in Your love for me, fill me to
overflowing. In Jesus' name. Amen.*

The Perfect Ending

May the Lord direct your hearts into God's love
and Christ's perseverance.

2 THESSALONIANS 3:5

*W*e don't have a GPS that can lead us away from our fleshly desires and into the heart of God. We can't get there on our own. Only the Spirit of God can take us there. Only through God's Spirit can we leave behind our sin condition, our tendency to succumb to peer pressure, our focus on our own needs, our desire to be loved on our terms.

In God's great mercy and grace, He allows us to bask in His love. And in that place He also gives us the strength to continue when our way grows difficult. In the refreshing coolness of God's presence we receive His reassurance of our value. He names us Hephzibah and Beulah: "For the LORD will take delight in you, and your land will be married."

Truth is stranger than fiction! Every fairy tale written with promises of a knight coming to take away a maiden fair pales in comparison to the truth that a Prince will come—the King of kings and the Lord of lords—to carry us to His Father's house (John 14:2). And there we will be with Him, experiencing His presence and pure love untainted by our human limitations forever and ever. Until then we wait with full hearts, persevering because the end is worth waiting for.

What is your expectation of being in God's presence forever? Where do you place your hope for a future filled with love?

Dear heavenly Father, I look forward to the day when I will truly be one with You. Until that day comes, lead me into Your presence by Your Spirit. Fill me with You again and again. In Jesus' name. Amen.

Michelle McKinney Hammond

a writer, singer, and speaker who focuses on improving love-driven relationships, is the founder and president of HeartWing Ministries. She cohosted the Emmy-nominated show *Aspiring Women* for 10 years. Michelle is the bestselling author of *101 Ways to Get and Keep His Attention, Secrets of an Irresistible Woman, What to Do Until Love Finds You,* and *The Power of Being a Woman.*

To contact Michelle McKinney Hammond
or to get information on booking her for a speaking
engagement, please log on to

www.michellehammond.com

More Encouraging Books by

Michelle McKinney Hammond

101 Ways to Get and Keep His Attention

The DIVA Principle

How to Avoid the 10 Mistakes Single Women Make

How to Be Found by the Man You've Been Looking For

How to Get Past Disappointment

The Power of Being a Woman

Right Attitudes for Right Living

A Sassy Girl's Guide to Loving God

Sassy, Single, and Satisfied

Secrets of an Irresistible Woman

What to Do Until Love Finds You

Why Do I Say "Yes" When I Need to Say "No"?

A Woman's Gotta Do What a Woman's Gotta Do

DVD by Michelle

How to Get Past Disappointment (180 min.)

How to Be Found by the Man You've Been Looking For

Dynamic and down-to-earth relationship expert Michelle McKinney Hammond shares a fresh, new perspective on dating, mating, and relating. She's packed this hands-on, straightforward book with powerful insights, wisdom born of experience, and practical advice to help you attract, evaluate, communicate with, and love your future mate. She encourages you to...

- take your life off hold and live purposefully
- gain a better understanding of men
- get ready for love spiritually, emotionally, and physically
- let go of dead-end relationships
- learn how to recognize your Mr. Right and capture his heart

In her candid, upbeat style, Michelle uses the biblical story of Ruth and Boaz to reveal that finding a life partner can be a vibrant time of embracing where you are and becoming the woman who will attract the love you've always wanted.

A Woman's Gotta Do
What a Woman's Gotta Do

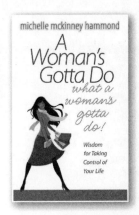

Are you ready for a lively journey? Packed with upbeat and inspiring stories, Michelle explores the wisdom of Proverbs 31 and offers intriguing questions to help you learn more about who you are and where you're going. You'll discover keys to...

- exploring and enjoying every aspect of the season of life you're in
- live up to your full potential and be who God created you to be
- have a greater, more positive impact on people around you

With enthusiasm and plenty of encouragement, Michelle offers biblical truths and valuable insights to help you grow spiritually strong and make your life more dynamic.

How to Get Past Disappointment

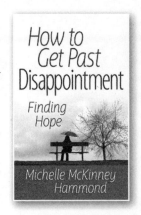

The Samaritan woman always welcomed the heat of the sun once she sat on the edge of the well and splashed her face with cool water from the bucket she drew up. This place was her oasis of peace and refreshing. But not today. A stranger was sitting in her spot. A Jewish rabbi…

Drawing on the dramatic story of the "Woman at the Well," Michelle offers an unforgettable encounter with God to help you move beyond disappointment and experience joy. Through powerful biblical teaching, she reveals how to…

- let God's love help you face your hurts and forgive when necessary
- embrace new beginnings
- release your expectations and embrace God's blessings

You can experience God's love more fully and live the life He wants you to have.

Also available: How to Get Past Disappointment DVD!
Let Michelle lead your group in six dynamic, 30-minute sessions.